The

ABC's
of
Home Food
Dehydration

The
ABC's
of
Home Food
Dehydration

*

Barbara Densley

ISBN 13: 978-0-88290-051-3

Published by Horizon Publishers, an imprint of Cedar Fort, Inc.
2373 W. 700 S., Springville, UT, 84663
Distributed by Cedar Fort, Inc., www.cedarfort.com

Cover design by Angela Olsen
Cover design © 2007 by Lyle Mortimer

Printed in the United States of America

10 9 8 7 6 5 4 3 2

Printed on acid-free paper

THIS BOOK IS BROUGHT TO YOU WITH LOVE

FROM

BARBARA DENSLEY

AND HER TASTE TESTING CRITICS—

KEN, ROSEMARIE, KELLY, KENNY,
DEIDRA, AND CARLY

ABOUT THE AUTHOR

Barbara Maynard Densley, author of *The ABC's of Home Food Dehydrating*, is a woman who has answers to many commonly-asked questions on food preservation. When others couldn't supply the answers to these queries, she immersed herself in experimentation and learned for herself. Now it is not uncommon for college professors in the nutrition-related fields to direct others to her because of her insight and knowledge in the field of food preservation.

She was raised in Salt Lake City, Utah. After her marriage to Kenneth Densley, the couple moved to Logan, Utah. He worked on his degree; she worked for the Extension Service, the Dairy Industry Department and the Dairy Council of Utah. Military service and Ken's advanced schooling took the couple to Georgia, Texas, Utah, and then to Carmichael, California, their present home. They are the parents of three children.

Interest in cooking and food preservation techniques has continued throughout Barbara's adult life. Early in her marriage her Pineapple Upside Down Cake and Cheese Muffins won ribbons at food fairs, which stimulated enthusiasm. A calling to teach ladies in her church group about nutrition and food storage channeled her experience in new directions. She compiled a recipe book showing how to use storage foods, and co-authored a textured vegetable protein recipe book—this led her into the writing field. She began attending seminars, adult education classes, and workshops on foods and nutrition. Soon she was teaching and lecturing on food preservation, with emphasis on food dehydration. She has conducted classes for garden clubs, church groups from many faiths, sewing circles, co-ops, the YWCA, and groups formed by home economists in her area.

Not being content to leave questions unanswered, she has experimented and innovated, becoming a leader in the field of food dehydration and a forthright advocate of the art of home food preservation.

Horizon Publishers is pleased to publish her book, *The ABC's of Home Food Dehydrating*, for we recognize that it contains useful information, not available elsewhere, that will add to the body of knowledge in this rapidly-expanding field.

FOREWORD

I am writing this book at the request of many friends that are interested in knowing more about my new venture with food dehydrating.

My family loves fruit leather. I used to make it by the trayful. I would carry out the cookie sheets, stack them one on top of another crisscrossed for circulation to about one foot high, and then proceed to find four props that would stand taller than my stack. I would drape cheesecloth over the top carefully so I didn't let it drop into the top pan of leather. Then I would attach clothespins to the corners to anchor the cloth so it would not blow off or into the leather; but would protect the leather from stray cats, birds, bees, flies, etc. Come evening, I would cart all of my paraphernalia back into the house to prevent nighttime moisture absorption from defeating the daytime evaporation. The next morning, out it would all go with cautions that no water sprinklers be turned on until the leather was dry. Each night I would sigh, "There must be a better way!" Then I happened upon a food dehydrator and what joy! My husband calls it "my new toy." I must agree that I am enjoying my dehydrating experiences—just like a child with a new plaything.

When I first got my dehydrator there wasn't very much information available about dehydration. After World War II, victory gardens ceased, and so did work with dehydration. Just recently this old/new method of food preservation has been revived, but there is so very much to be learned. There are so many unanswered questions. Recently published information contains many discrepancies. One book will say soak the food overnight to rehydrate, the next book will say soak the food for 2 hours.

Step by step through the dehydrating processes these discrepancies exist. I became frustrated and decided that climate and heat source determine to some extent the outcome of successful or unsuccessful dehydration procedures, but that it was going to take a lot of experimentation to get the answers to my many questions.

My questions started the day I bought my commercially-made home dehydrator: how big should I cut the fruit slices, should I pretreat fruit and vegetables, how should I pretreat, how long should it take for them to dry, how should I store them, how much moisture should I use to reconstitute them, where would I find recipes for use of the dehydrated fruit and vegetables? These questions continued on and on. I started to make notes, I changed my notes again, and again. I am still changing my notes.

Dehydration is interesting and challenging. I have found that dehydrating and the use of dehydrated foods is a very enjoyable and rewarding experience.

I would like to express my appreciation to the many people who have shared their dehydrating experiences, ideas, and recipes with me.

I sincerely hope this book will be a useful guide and will lead you to a new and challenging venture with dehydration.

TABLE OF CONTENTS

CHAPTER I

DRY FOOD! WHY?

Many people ask, "Why should we dry food?" There are many advantages in drying foods. To mention a few:

Nutritious Foods

Fresh fruits and vegetables are our richest source of nutrients. Properly prepared dried foods that are stored carefully and reconstituted correctly are the next best source of nutrients. The vitamin A and C content is lowered in dried foods because they are sensitive to heat, light, and air. Even carefully prepared fresh produce loses some of the A and C vitamins. Because the water is removed from dehydrated food, the remaining food has more concentrated nutrients. Dehydrated foods are a good source for minerals. The bulk and energy supplied by food is not affected by dehydration.

Home preserved food that has been preserved at peak harvest time without time lapse before processing retains more nutrients and flavor. Even best quality fruits and vegetables rarely stand up well under bulk harvesting, processing, and transportation conditions.

Some foods are better dried than frozen or canned. Dehydrated food is good natural food with no preservatives added. Fruit leather is an excellent substitute for candy with no question as to nutritional value.

What's That Word We Hear So Often? Economy!

Webster says, "Economy—thrifty administration; often, retrenchment in expenditure; strict husbanding of resources."

Retrench the food budget! That sounds like an excellent idea, but how? A vegetable garden in a corner of the yard. Dwarf fruit trees in tubs. Herb gardens in planters. Perhaps it isn't feasible to grow fruits and vegetables.

Another possibility is purchasing fresh-picked fruits and vegetables from a nearby farm. By purchasing "in season" the produce will be less costly and more nutritious.

If a family can use 20 pounds of potatoes before they spoil, they can save money over buying 10 pounds. However, many families cannot consume the larger quantities before spoilage. With a dehydrator it is possible to purchase the larger quantity at a savings and then dehydrate the excess.

Another example is dehydrated herbs. Even to purchase parsley from the market and dehydrate it saves money. A sprig of parsley can be purchased for about 20 cents. After dehydrating it, it will fill a 49 cent parsley flake container three times. This results in a savings of $1.27. Home grown herbs would save even more.

It is not necessary to use sugar to preserve dried fruit. This in and of itself is quite a savings. It is not necessary to purchase bottles and lids. This is an advantage over wet pack preservation. Bags or containers for freezer foods are expensive. The electricity for keeping the foods frozen until they are ready for use adds to the expense also.

Dehydration does help with the thrifty administration of the food budget.

Battle of the Bulge

The freezer is bulging! The shelves are overflowing! There isn't room to store another thing! Does that sound familiar? There is no need for such exclamations with dehydrated foods.

Sixty ten-inch ears of corn cut off from the cob will store in a one gallon plastic bottle. Foods with natural sugar do not reduce as much as vegetables, but there is still a big difference over wet pack or frozen foods. The dried product varies from one-fifth to one-tenth of the weight of fresh food. Because of this reduction in bulk, it makes dried food ideal for camping, back packing, and home storage—especially in homes with limited storage space.

Do-It-Yourself Convenience Foods

Economy—high nutrition—convenience food, what a combination! All of this is available with dehydration.

Purchase mushrooms when they are a leader item in the market and dehydrate them for use when the price is high. No dashing out to purchase them at the last minute because a recipe calls for mushrooms.

Buy a round steak next time it is on special, and make beef jerky. What a convenience for the back packer, skier and camper.

Left-over chicken from Sunday dinner may be dehydrated as a convenience food. Unexpected guests have a treat when served chicken a la king and it is great for campers.

Onions may be purchased in quantity at a reduced cost and dehydrated to be used as a convenience food.

To get the grater out to grate carrots, potatoes, zucchini, apples, etc. is always inconvenient and seems like a waste of time and effort for just one salad or just one cake. With a dehydrator, grate away and dry the excess for future convenience food. Carrot cake, zucchini bread, carrot-jello salad, apple cake and boiled puddings can be made by reconstituting the fruit or vegetable for five minutes. No muss or fuss to clean the grater each and every time.

A skier's delight is a roll of fruit leather tucked in a pocket to provide quick energy. Banana leather, made from trimmer bananas, is delicious and economical.

Seasoning mixes, potatoes, jerky, fruit rolls, etc. can be made at home for a fraction of the cost of purchased convenience foods.

Just For Fun

It is fun to raise, harvest and dehydrate food. It is fascinating to watch the vegetables and fruits shrivel, shrink, and deform. It is amazing to reconstitute them and watch them plump up and return to their original form. It is a delight to taste the fresh-picked flavor which is a distinct quality of dehydrated produce.

It is enjoyable to give fruit baskets filled with delicious home dehydrated delicacies and answer queries, "What is this?"—"Did you really do this?"—"Well, I didn't know you could make that!"

Some complain about the labor involved in raising and dehydrating vegetables and say it isn't worth it. It depends on where values are placed. There is no better way to relax and get back to nature than in exercising the body by working in the garden. It relieves the tensions built up by competing in a busy, fast-paced world. Does sitting on a bicycle pedaling away in the game room to burn up calories compare with cultivating the vegetable garden or picking the berries? To some the answer is yes; and to others it is no.

Grandmother successfully met the challenge of dehydrating food in her day. With the present day modern convenience of a food dehydrator, the challenge of preserving food by dehydration is being revived. Food dehydration is an inexpensive, convenient, and nutritious way to preserve excess food and prevent waste.

CHAPTER II

DRYING METHODS AND TECHNIQUES

Drying is an excellent natural method of preserving fruits and vegetables. There are many ways of drying produce. A discussion of the many methods will help the reader determine which method best suits individual requirements.

Attic Drying

Attic drying is a method in which foods are suspended in a warm area. Vegetable or fruit slices are threaded on string and hung in a warm, insect-free attic, porch, or above a cook-stove.

Most produce can be dried in the attic. Ideal conditions, however, require a proper balance of heat and air movement to produce a quality product. Adding a fan to the attic heat may help circulate the air, making the process more efficient.

String beans may be threaded onto a string and hung in the attic. When they are dried this way they are called "leather britches."

Drill a hole in cobs of corn, thread them on a string, and hang them in the attic. This corn is excellent when it is parched.

Tie a small bunch of herbs tightly with a strong string. Hang them upside-down in the attic to dry.

Slice apples in 1/4-inch rings, thread them onto heavy string, and place them in the attic to dry. Leave ample space between the slices for air circulation.

Cloth Bag Drying

Produce with green color or delicate-flavored herbs should not be dried in the sun because they lose chlorophyll and oil. Cloth bag drying is an easy way to overcome this problem.

Peaches, apples, pears, etc. may be cut into 3/8-inch slices, put into a cloth bag, and hung on a clothesline to dry. It is necessary to shake the bag several times a day to keep the air circulating and to stir the fruit for more even drying. The material for the bag should be loosely woven to allow air movement, but tight enough to prevent insect infestation.

If the temperature varies over 20° between day and night, high condensation will occur, making it necessary to move the drying food inside at night. When drying in a cloth bag it is also necessary to protect the food from rain.

To dry dill, clip the stock when the seed pod starts to open, place the stock into a cloth bag, hang on the clothesline in the shade, and dry. As the seeds dry they fall into the bottom of the bag to make dill seed. The stocks are used as dillweed.

Produce dried in this manner loses some color and flavor but it is a good substitute when a dehydrator is not available.

Drying on the Plant

Some things are best dried on the plant. Fava beans, lima beans, navy beans, pinto beans, kidney beans, soy beans, and black eyed peas are good examples.

When the bean pod turns light brown, the seed is mature and should be harvested. If left too long, the pod will split open and allow the seeds to fall on the ground. Pick the pods or cut the vines, place them in a cloth sack, tie a knot in the end, and hang them where they get good air circulation to thoroughly dry. Shake the bag, stomp on it, or beat it with a mallet to shell the beans from the pods. Shake the bag, untie the top, remove the pods from the top of the sack, and then pour the beans into a container. On the next windy day, pour the beans from one container to another, and let the wind blow the chaff away.

Before storing the beans, precautions should be taken to prevent development of any insect eggs that my have gotten onto the beans while they were drying. This can be accomplished by placing the dried beans into the deepfreeze at 0° F. for 48 hours. The beans may then be placed in insect-proof containers and stored in a cool, dry place. If a deepfreeze is not available, the beans may be pasteurized by placing them in a preheated oven at 175° F. for 15 minutes. Make sure the beans are spread in a thin layer so that the heat reaches each bean. Some nutrition is lost with this method because of the high temperature but it is necessary to kill the eggs. When a deepfreeze is not available, this is the next best precaution to guard against infestation.

Corn may be dried on the stalk. When the husk is crisp and the stocks have lost their chlorophyll, the corn is mature. Pick the corn, remove the husk, and place in bags or on screens to continue air circulation for thorough drying. It is necessary to protect the corn from rodents. The corn may be stored on the cob, but to save space it should be shelled and stored in a moisture-proof container. To shell the corn, hold the cob in both hands and twist in opposite directions. Have a container available to catch the falling kernels. It may be necessary to wind-blow the corn to remove cob chaff. Parched corn is a good snack food. If the corn is ground in a mill, it makes a good cornmeal.

Popcorn should be harvested the same way. The unpopped kernels of popcorn make a delicious breakfast cereal when coarse-ground through a mill and served with cream and sugar.

Oven Drying

Fruits and vegetables may be dried in the oven. It is important to place a thermometer in the oven to determine the temperature of the bottom, middle, and top racks. The temperature should not be allowed to go over 140° F. It will be necessary to prop the door open to assure proper temperature level. When the temperature goes over 140° F., nutrition is lost and the end product is not as good. With an electric oven, a fan placed to blow into the oven helps air circulation and causes moisture to be removed from the oven.

The pilot light in a gas oven gives about the right temperature, but without air circulation it is not efficient. The fan cannot be used because it will blow out the pilot light. It is necessary to set the oven at its lowest temperature range. Check the temperature in all three rack areas. Block the door open to reduce the heat and increase the air movement.

Special trays may be constructed to fit the oven. Use clean, dry wood that is free from pitch and odors. The trays may be made of 1/4-inch-wide slats spaced 1/2-inch apart, or made from stainless steel hardware cloth. Simple nylon-net-covered shelves may also be used. Separate the trays of food by about 2-1/2-inches. Leave about a 1-1/2-inch clearance from the oven walls, and about a 3-inch clearance from the top and bottom of the oven. The food should be spread only one layer deep for better circulation. Stir the food and rotate the trays for more even drying. To prevent scorching, check the food often, especially near the end of the drying time. The time required for drying is determined by the type of food, size of the pieces, the size of the load on the tray, and the humidity.

Black Mission figs have a distinctive flavor. Allow the figs to remain on the trees until they drop to the ground. A sheet may be placed beneath the tree to catch the figs. When the figs drop, it indicates they have a high sugar content and will make a good dried product.

Dip figs into boiling water for 1 minute to craze the skin. Drip dry on absorbent toweling, place on oven racks (specially constructed), place in the oven with the temperature as low as possible, place a fan so a gentle flow of air circulates around the fruit in the oven, and prop the oven door open about 3-inches to maintain a temperature of 140° F. Dry the figs until they are leathery on the outside. The interior will be slightly sticky, but free of juice. Store dried figs in plastic bags in metal shortening cans with tight-fitting lids. Place masking tape around the lid of the can to give an airtight seal. Be sure to keep the dried food in a cool, dry place.

A big disadvantage to oven drying is the cost factor. It is also very inconvenient to not have the oven available for baking needs when it is being used to dehydrate food. Another disadvantage is the unnecessary heat in the home caused by having the oven operating on a continuous basis during hot weather. Because it is hard to control the temperature, there is a greater loss of nutrients and flavor.

Warning: Never leave home with food drying in the oven when it is possible for the trays or the covering to catch fire. If fire should occur, close the oven door and turn off the heat immediately; lack of oxygen will extinguish the fire.

Solar Dryer

A solar dryer will dry food faster than just placing it in open air. It costs nothing to operate it if it is built without a fan.

The principle behind a solar dryer is the greenhouse offect created by the sun's rays passing through glass or plastic—the energy is absorbed by the interior of the dryer, thereby raising the temperature. This dryer would be more efficient with a fan. Fan motors draw a small amount of electric current when compared to a heating element.

If desired, the sun's rays may be intensified by appropriately placing a mirror to direct additional rays to the solar pane. If this is done, caution must be taken to see that the inside temperature of the dryer does not exceed 140° F. Such heat temperatures are easily attained in sunny dry climates—even without a mirror.

The solar dryer is a box with one surface being glass or plastic. Vents are necessary to permit escape of moisture by natural air movement, or by forced air when a fan is added. Place screens over the vents to protect the food from insects and animals. The box may be made from any appropriate building material such as masonite or plywood. For safety, it is advisable to use plastic for the pane rather than glass.

Sun Drying

Sun drying is probably the oldest method known for preserving foods. Fruits, meats, and vegetables that are exposed to the sun and wind just naturally shrivel and dry.

For successful sun drying of vegetables, temperatures of 100° F. or above are preferred. A low relative humidity is also desired. Lower temperatures are permissible for fruits because of their higher sugar content. Vegetables must be cut into small sizes for more rapid drying. Vegetables are not as good as fruits when they are dried in the sun because they lose flavor and color. Sun drying is a race between mold and a quality dried product.

Such fruits as nectarines, apples, pears, apricots, and peaches turn brown when they are exposed to air. This oxidation process robs the fruit of vitamin C and flavor. To stop this chemical reaction so that home dried fruits will be as appetizing as purchased fruit, it is necessary to treat the fruits with sulfur. To maintain an appetizing product, most commercial food drying companies use sulfur in drying, and nitrogen in packaging.

If properly used, the sulfuring technique is safe. Sulfur prevents browning and formation of air-pockets, repels insects, speeds up drying time, and is a preservative. Sulfuring fruit does not prevent insect infestation during storage.

General Instructions for Sun Dried Sulfuring

A sulfuring box is required. Always sulfur outdoors. Do not breath sulfur. Do not plan to dry sulfured fruit in the oven. Garden dusting sulfur should not be used. Use pure powdered sulfur or flowers of sulfur; check to be sure that it is 99.8 percent pure. Sulfur with impurities will not burn properly.

Use slatted wooden trays for sulfuring. Packing crates may be reconstructed to make good trays. Do not use yellow pine or any wood with a lot of pitch. Do not use aromatic woods such as cedar or redwood.

Do not use iron, steel or aluminum for trays. When they are exposed to the burning sulfur, iron and aluminum sulfide is formed which gives a bad appearance and a metal taste to the fruit. Zinc poisoning is rare with fruits, but can happen if sulfured fruit is placed on zinc hardware cloth. Zinc is used by the body, but excessive amounts result in diarrhea. Plastic screening should not be placed too close to the heat source. Unless fiberglas screening has been teflon coated, unraveled bits of fiberglas can get into the fruit. Stainless steel hardware cloth is preferred but expensive; therefore, wood is recommended as best for sulfuring.

Step by Step Procedure:

1. Assemble all of the required materials before preparing fruit.

2. Determine the amount of sulfur required. An 8-inch aluminum pie plate makes a good container. (See Table 1 for sulfuring amounts and times.)

3. Place fruits in a single layer with cut surface up to retain juices.

4. Stack trays with a 1-1/2-inch block at each corner for separation to allow the sulfur fumes to circulate freely. The trays should be raised with blocks (bricks are good to use) to 10-inches above the sulfur container to prevent the trays from being scorched by the burning sulfur. If a lot of fruit is to be dried, then it is advisable to build a rack on 10-inch legs to hold the trays. See diagram on page 10.

5. Cover the stack of trays with a large cardboard packing carton. Choose one large enough to allow a 1-1/2 inch clearance on three sides of the stack, and allow about 8-inches on the side where the sulfur pan is to be placed. (Prevents scorching of the trays.) The carton should be airtight. Small holes or cracks may be covered with masking tape. Cut a flap in the end at the bottom of the carton, and make another flap on the opposite end of the carton at the top. The bottom flap allows the sulfur to be lighted, and the top flap controls circulation of sulfur fumes.

6. Place the pan of sulfur under the box near the opening, but make sure it is far enough away from the stack and the side of the carton that it will not burn either of them. Do not leave burned matches in the container because they may prevent the sulphur from burning to completion. The burning time of the sulfur varies

SULFURING RACK

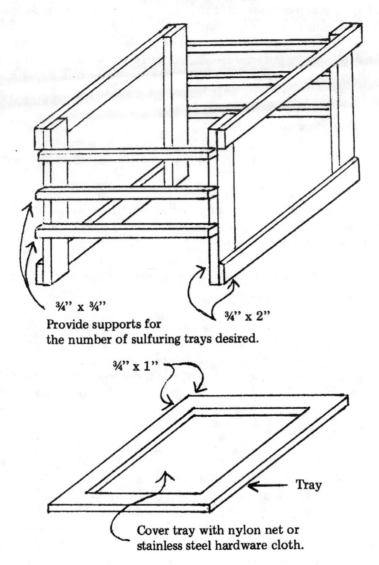

¾" x ¾"
Provide supports for
the number of sulfuring trays desired.

¾" x 2"

¾" x 1"

Tray

Cover tray with nylon net or
stainless steel hardware cloth.

with ventilation, shape of the container, weather conditions, etc.
Tests show that 2 cups of sulfur will burn approximately 2 hours.
Turn the bottom flaps of the carton out, and weight the flaps with
a brick to seal.

7. Open the two small flaps. Light the sulfur with a match.
After 5 minutes, check the bottom flap to see that the sulfur is

burning well; if not, light it again. When the sulfur is burning, close both flaps. Keep children and pets away from the irritating fumes of the sulfur. It is best to begin sulfuring in the early evening so the fruit can remain in the box overnight. The fruit can only absorb a limited quantity of sulfur so there is no cause for concern about over-sulfuring.

8. As soon as the dew dries the following morning, move the trays to a place with direct sunlight. The trays should stand at least 2-inches off from the ground to allow for air circulation. Do not place them near a busy street to avoid lead deposits from automobile exhausts accumulating on the fruit. Place netting over the fruit but do not let it lay on the fruit. This will protect the fruit from insects and blowing dust and leaves. Protect the fruit from evening dew. Continue the drying process for 2 to 3 days.

9. When the fruit is soft, leathery and pliable, it is dry. Let the fruit cool before packaging. As soon as the fruit is dry, pack it into scalded, dry, insect-proof containers. Store the dried fruits in a dry, cool place away from light. Plastic or glass jars are very good storage containers. Protect the sulfured fruit from metal reaction by placing plastic wrap under the lid. Shortening cans or coffee cans may be used if the fruit is placed in a plastic bag first. Freezer bags are suitable for fruit stored in the freezer; however, they are not recommended for shelf storage because insects can chew through the plastic.

10. Remember, sulfuring fruit does not prevent insect infestation. Fruits should also be treated as described previously under, "Dried on the Plant" beans.

A disadvantage of sun drying is the inconvenience of having to move the food each night or cover it. Precautions must be taken to guard against insects, dust, rain, and animals.

For some people the taste and odor of sulfured fruit is undesirable. With the constant temperature and airflow provided by a heating element and fan in a dehydrator, drying time is accelerated; thereby, reducing the need for sulfuring.

Table 1. SUN DRIED FRUIT SULFURING CHART

FRUIT	PREPARATION GUIDE	AMOUNT OF SULFUR	TIME
Apples	Wash, peel, core, and cut into 3/8-inch slices or rings.	Use 2 teaspoons of sulfur for each pound of prepared fruit.	45 minutes
Apricots	Wash, cut in halves, and remove pits.	Use 1 teaspoon of sulfur for each pound of pre-pared fruit.	2 hours
Nectarines	Wash, peel if desired, cut in halves, and remove pits.	Use 2 teaspoons of sulfur for each pound of pre-pared fruit.	2 to 3 hours
Peaches	Wash, peel if desired, cut in halves, and remove pits.	Use 2 teaspoons of sulfur for each pound of pre-pared fruit.	2 to 3 hours
Pears	Wash, cut in half, core, and peel.	Use 2-1/2-teaspoons of sulfur for each pound of prepared fruit.	5 hours

CHAPTER III

SELECTING A HOME FOOD DEHYDRATOR

"This is the best dehydrator on the market!" Ever heard that statement before? In 1974 there were only about a half-a-dozen companies claiming the honor, but today the market is deluged!

Home Made Units

In competition with the commercially-made home dehydrator is the "Do-It-Yourself" unit. Some people experience success with homemade units. Others decide (after many hours consumed in searching for the right kind of materials, learning of the expense involved to purchase the materials, and determining the hours of labor required to construct the unit) that they would never undertake the project. Sometimes the homemade unit is successful. Sometimes it is a failure. In either case, the recommendation is usually "Don't do it."—before their project was completed, it cost more and took more time than they had anticipated.

To avid "Do-It-Yourselfers" however, time and money are immaterial; it is the challenge to succeed that is important. The following guidelines may be of value to the home builder.

1. Start far in advance of completion date to allow sufficient time to special order hard-to-find materials.

2. Research and study to discover the safest materials available for use in construction.

3. Don't give up experimenting until the proper air flow and temperature requirements are achieved.

4. Patent rights permit building one dehydrator for self use. They do not allow someone to go into production using a design the manufacturer has spent time and money perfecting or the manufacturer may take legal action.

Choose the Dehydrator that Meets Your Needs

Now, back to the dehydrator—a "best" dehydrator does not exist for all people. The manufacturers have designed their dehydrators with the features they believed the consumer would consider the most important. Because individual needs and preferences vary, each person requires different features in a dehydrator. The following guidelines may be helpful in choosing or building a dehydrator.

It may be desirable to prepare a chart of features and assign a rank of 1, 2, and 3 to each important feature using 3 as the most important. It is then possible to review the features of the available dehydrators assigning 0 if the feature doesn't exist, 1 if the feature is present but of little value, and a 2 or 3 as appropriate if the features are of more importance. The dehydrator with the highest score would be the dehydrator that best fits the individual's requirements.

Exterior Walls:

1. Transparent wall or door for viewing and/or sun dehydration.

2. Walls that are insulated to prevent heat loss.

3. Durability.

4. Attractiveness.

5. Easy cleaning.

The higher the insulating quality of the sidewall construction the more the heat will be retained and used for the dehydration of food rather than warming the air surrounding the dehydrator. Selection of materials high in insulating quality, however, may not provide the most durable surface. Aluminum or steel walls would be durable, but will transfer heat to the outside of the dehydrator as they are conductors rather than insulators. As with many dehydrator features, wall selection may require a compromise to meet the individual's preferences.

Heating Unit:

1. *Safety.* The element should be located where dripping juices or dried material will not fall on the element creating a fire hazard.

Does the location of the element create a shock or burn hazard?

2. *Size.* Is the element wattage appropriate for the dehydrator size?

If fan capacity is high and the element wattage is small, the dehydrator may not be able to maintain adequate dehydration temperature.

Proper element size requires a balance between air flow and heating capacity.

3. *User serviceability:* Ease in obtaining and replacing heating element.

Fan:

1. *Noise of operation.* A squirrel cage fan operates more quietly than blade fans.

2. *Size.* Inadequate air movement will reduce drying speed. Too much air movement capacity will cause unnecessary heat loss from the dehydrator, wasting energy.

Thermostat or Thermoswitch:

1. *Thermostat* may be set to any of a range of temperatures. This feature is advantageous due to desired heat selection for such items as herbs requiring a low temperature setting and beef jerky requiring a high temperature setting.

2. A *thermoswitch* is a preset switch that maintains a constant temperature at a setting established by the manufacturer. This setting may be high enough to case harden some foods and actually decrease the efficiency of the dehydrator. It does not provide the user with a choice of settings.

3. Some dehydrators do not have thermostats or thermoswitches but do offer the user a variety of heating element sizes for different dehydrating temperatures to accommodate different foods such as jerky.

Shelf Material:

1. *Stainless steel.* This is the preferred shelf material. However, it is expensive and to date unavailable in any manufactured home dehydrator. (To the author's knowledge.)

2. *Hardware cloth*. Most building material supply houses carry hardware cloth that is cadmium coated. This material can create a health hazard. Avoid it.

3. *Fiberglas*. Fiberglas should be teflon coated. Even when teflon coated, the woven strands can separate and adhere to dehydrated food creating a health hazard.

Fiberglas shelves also sag with use, permitting food trays to touch trays below, creating a problem in tray removal and dehydrating efficiency.

4. *Plastic*. Make sure that plastic shelving was created for dehydrator use and is food safe at the dehydrator operating temperature.

5. *Nylon screening*. Unsuitable due to stretching and sagging at dehydrating temperatures.

6. *Aluminum*. May leave a noticeable taste and an undesirable staining on the food. Acid fruits and sulfur will cause pitting.

7. *Wood*. Difficult to clean, therefore bacterial growth may become a problem. Moist foods cause warping and splintering. Heating elements may scorch wood and create a fire hazard. Many woods cause an undesirable odor and flavor change.

Capacity:

1. *Tray surface area*. The surface area of the trays create the drying capacity, not the cubic footage of the interior of the dehydrator.

2. Capacity must not be confused with production ability. A dehydrator may in fact hold more food but dehydrate more slowly because of inadequate heat and airflow.

3. *Economy*. Select a unit adequate to the family needs. A large unit is by necessity more expensive, yet it may not be needed by the family. Purchasing an oversize unit will cost more to operate and is a waste of energy if the majority of the time it is operating with partially-filled trays.

CHAPTER IV

UNDERSTANDING THE DRYING PROCESS

To understand the drying process, it is desirable to know what takes place with food after it is harvested.

Enzyme Action

To preserve produce it is necessary to stop enzyme action and prevent yeasts, molds, and bacteria from growing or multiplying. Dehydrating food removes enough of the products' natural moisture to prevent enzyme action and decomposition.

Webster says: "Enzyme—A complex mostly protein product of living cells that induces or speeds chemical reactions in plants and animals without being itself permanently altered."

Enzymes are made by living cells. They speed up the chemical reaction that would take place over a longer period of time without their presence. They act as a catalyst to break down complex substances into simple ones without being changed themselves. More than 1,000 types of enzymes are in our bodies, and each one performs only one specific function. Enzymes can be destroyed by temperatures over 140° F.

For an example of enzyme action at work, let's take fresh picked corn. If it is steamed immediately after picking, it is sweet; but if it is picked and not steamed, much of the sugar turns to starch. In an experiment with two cobs of corn, one cob was steamed and dried, the other was not steamed but just dried. The result: the unsteamed cob continued to get more starchy and flavorless each day while the steamed cob had the enzyme action stopped. When the first cob was reconstituted by adding boiling water, it was like fresh picked corn ready to cook. Because the enzyme action was not stopped by steaming, it changed the color, texture, and flavor of the second cob and made it unappetizing.

Another example is pineapple. The pineapple was not steamed, but just sliced into tidbit size pieces, placed on trays, and dehydrated. As the water evaporated out of the pineapple the enzyme action was suspended. When it was reconstituted, the pineapple (because it was not heated over 140° F. to stop enzyme action) had to be treated like fresh pineapple. The moisture started the enzyme action again. Dehydrated pineapple that has not been steamed cannot be used in gelatin salad because the gelatin will not set. In contrast, canned pineapple will set in a gelatin salad because its enzyme action was stopped in the canning process.

pH Factor

For dehydrating it is helpful to understand how the pH factor and heat control the growth of micro-organisms. The amount of acid a food contains determines the precautions required to safely preserve it.

Acid is measured on a pH scale with strong-acid being 1, neutral 7, and strong-alkali 14. (Refer to Table 2.)

The strong-acid fruits may be safely canned in a boiling water bath at 212° F. It is necessary to guard against heat resistant bacteria and toxins with low-acid/nonacid foods. It requires a pressure canner to raise the temperature to $240\text{-}250^{\circ}$ F. to safely can vegetables, fish, and meat.

Table 2 shows that the strength of the acid determines which micro-organisms grow. Heat is the controlling factor of enzyme action. The temperature of the dehydrator is sufficient to suspend the action in strong-acid fruits, but it is necessary to steam blanch the low-acid vegetables.

Micro-organisms

Micro-organisms cannot grow in food when sufficient moisture has been removed. It is important not to allow wet food to stand in large batches while still warm from blanching. Cool rapidly! Do not let fruits or vegetables stand at room temperature for long periods of time when rehydrating.

Moisture in food supports the growth of fungi and bacteria that bring about the decomposition of food. With the right combination of heat and air to remove the moisture, dehydration takes place before the produce can spoil.

Water Content of Dehydrated Foods

The water content of properly dried vegetables should be five percent or less. Fruits may contain from five percent to twenty percent moisture, depending on the desired use. For long time storage when the fruit is to be used in cooked recipes, five percent moisture content is best. For snacks, twenty percent moisture content makes the fruit juicy and delicious; but the shelf life isn't

Table 2. pH SCALE

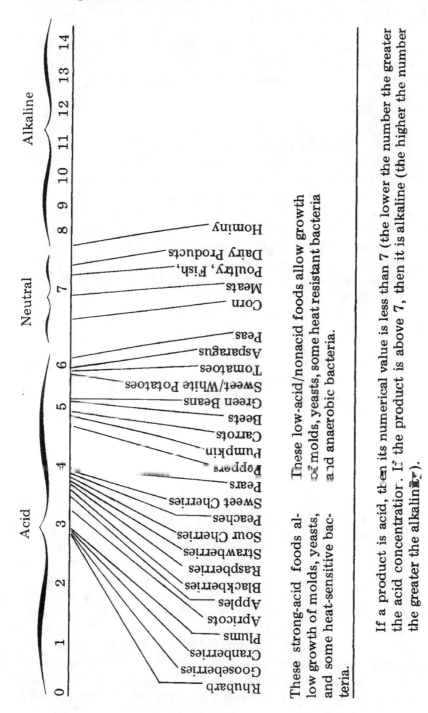

Alkaline

Neutral

Acid

| 0 | 1 | 2 | 3 | 4 | 5 | 6 | 7 | 8 | 9 | 10 | 11 | 12 | 13 | 14 |

Hominy
Dairy Products
Poultry, Fish,
Meats
Corn
Peas
Asparagus
Tomatoes
Sweet/White Potatoes
Green Beans
Beets
Carrots
Pumpkin
Poppers
Pears
Sweet Cherries
Peaches
Sour Cherries
Strawberries
Raspberries
Blackberries
Apples
Apricots
Plums
Cranberries
Gooseberries
Rhubarb

These strong-acid foods allow growth of molds, yeasts, and some heat-sensitive bacteria.

These low-acid/nonacid foods allow growth of molds, yeasts, some heat resistant bacteria and anaerobic bacteria.

If a product is acid, then its numerical value is less than 7 (the lower the number the greater the acid concentration. If the product is above 7, then it is alkaline (the higher the number the greater the alkalinity).

as long, and it should be stored in the refrigerator. As a rule, more moisture can be left in strong-acid fruits than in low-acid vegetables.

If non-acid meats and fish are heavily salted, they can safely contain more water than vegetables; but they should be kept in cold storage (40° F. or lower), and their storage life is shorter.

Case Hardening

Surface drying and souring may be prevented by controlling the temperature and airflow. Case hardening occurs when the temperature is too high and the heat hardens the outside of the produce, causing the moisture to be trapped inside. When this happens, bacteria grows and causes ruptured cells and flat-sour. If the temperature is too high, it can actually cook the produce and create an undesirable product because the cells are ruptured. Ruptured cells occur more in juicy foods. Flat-sour is more prevalent in firm vegetables, wax-coated fruits, and firm berries (grapes, cherries, blueberries).

High Humidity

High humidity affects dehydrating. If food has a high water content, it takes longer for it to dry. A combination of high water content in the food and a high humidity climate slows the drying process. It is important to understand the problem so care may be exercised to obtain a good end product.

When sun shines on moist food, evaporation takes place and the moisture in the food changes from a liquid to a vapor and moves up and away. This continues until all of the inside moisture has been moved out, resulting in dried food. When the outside air is humid, moisture in the food does not evaporate as rapidly, causing the drying process to take a longer time.

Dehydrators are affected by humidity also. Heat and air are required to accomplish dehydrating. The heating element causes the moisture in the product to change to vapor, and the fan blows the vapor out of the dryer through the vents. On high humidity days the process is slowed down. When the air has absorbed all of the moisture it can hold, the evaporation process stops unless the fan moves the air out. If the air outside of the dryer is as moist as the air inside of the dryer, it has no place to go. If the temperature in the dehydrator is raised to combat the problem, then case hardening is likely to occur. What is the solution? Cut foods smaller so they will dry faster. Put less food into the dryer. Puree fruit for leathers and store them in the deepfreeze to be dried at a later time. Equip the dehydrator with net or stainless steel shelves, and sulfur fruits to speed up the drying time. Of course, it is always possible to move to a hot and dry climate.

CHAPTER V

PRETREATMENT OF FOODS

The question is often asked, "Why is it necessary to pretreat fruits and vegetables before drying?"

Vitamins A and C

When dehydrating food, every precaution should be taken to preserve the nutrition of the food. Vitamins A and C are the two vitamins most affected by the drying process. By knowing this in advance, more care may be exercised in the preparation of foods with a high content of vitamin A and C. Before precaution may be exercised it is necessary to know how the drying process affects each of the vitamins, and which foods supply a rich source of these vitamins.

Vitamin A is a fat-soluble vitamin. It is not easily lost by ordinary cooking methods and does not dissolve out in cooking water. It is destroyed by oxidation, especially if heat is present, and it is unstable in light.

In its pure form vitamin A is a pale-yellow crystalline compound. It occurs naturally in animal fats. It is also supplied in the form of a provitamin known as the carotenes found in plants. It is converted into vitamin A by a chemical process believed to take place in the intestinal wall. It is abundant in dark green, leafy vegetables (the chlorophyll masks the yellow carotene), and in yellow vegetables.

Vitamin C is a water-soluble vitamin. It is very sensitive to oxygen, and is one of the least stable of vitamins. It can be lost through exposure to light, air, and heat. It is quite sensitive to alkalis. Soda should not be added to vitamin C foods to retain color when cooking because the alkalinity destroys the vitamin. Nonacid fruits and vegetables lose more ascorbic acid when heated than acid foods. Foods containing vitamin C should be kept under refrigeration to help preserve the vitamin. The taste of orange juice remains the same, but the vitamin C content decreases if the juice is not refrigerated and is exposed to heat and air. New freshly-harvested potatoes contain about 24 mg. of ascorbic acid per 100 Gm. After 3 months of storage the value has dropped to 12 mg. per 100 Gm., and after 6 months storage it has dropped to

8 mg. per 100 Gm. As much as 25 percent of the ascorbic acid may be lost from canned vegetables and fruits when they are stored at 80° F. for 1 year. To reduce the temperature to 65° F. the loss is only 10 percent. Therefore, it is wise to store dried food in a cool place.

Pretreatment Determines Food Value After Dehydration

Food may start out with a high vitamin content but much of it may be lost through processing. Harvesting many hours or even days before it is to be used, allowing food to stand at room temperature when it should be refrigerated, soaking the food in water rather than washing it quickly, overcooking, and not serving the food promptly after it is cooked all result in vitamin loss.

The pretreatment of food determines the nutritional value remaining in the food after dehydration. It is necessary to inactivate the enzymes by pretreatment, and to exercise precautions with regard to handling procedures to preserve vitamins and minerals as well as a high quality product. Unblanched vegetables will have poorer flavor and color after they have been dried. Strawberries lose their color and flavor in about 3 months if they are not pretreated.

Food processing for long storage, like canning, freezing, and dehydrating is a compromise between preventing spoilage and retaining vitamins. By cubing, soaking, blanching, and blending, the food has more of its surface exposed to oxidation and solubility. Therefore, it is only natural that those vitamins and minerals affected by these processes will suffer some loss. Choose first quality produce, handle with care, work rapidly while remembering the precautions required with individual foods, and maybe not all of the vitamin A and C will be preserved, but the food will run good competition with supermarket equivalents.

Table 3 shows a list of fruits and vegetables that are noted for their high vitamin A and C content. The food with the highest source is listed first, however, the foods listed are all good sources. Citrus fruits are not listed in the table because, as a rule, they are not dehydrated. When dehydrated fruit is pretreated with ascorbic acid, the vitamin C content is increased.

The steam blanching process required for vegetables will be explained in detail in the chapter on vegetable preparation.

Treatments to Preserve Vitamin C

The treatments that may be used to help preserve vitamin C are listed in alphabetical order for convenience as follows:

Table 3. FRUITS AND VEGETABLES CONTAINING HIGH AMOUNTS OF VITAMINS A AND C*

Fruits—Vitamin C
Apricots, dried, uncooked, sulfured
Cantaloupe (raw)
Mangos
Peaches, dried, uncooked, sulfured
Persimmons
Papayas
Cherries (red, sour)
Nectarines
Prunes, dried, uncooked

Fruits—Vitamin A
Strawberries (raw)
Mangos
Cantaloupe
Red Raspberries (raw)
Loganberries
Blackberries-Dewberries-Boysenberries
Black Raspberries (raw)
Peaches, dried, uncooked, sulfured
Pineapple (raw)
Blueberries
Apricots, dried, uncooked, sulfured
Persimmons

Vegetables—Vitamin C
Peppers (raw)
Broccoli
Kale
Brussels Sprouts
Cauliflower
Collards
Turnip Greens
Kohlrabi
Spinach
Mustard Greens
Cabbage
Asparagus
Dandelion Greens (raw)
Tomato Puree
New Potatoes
Tomato (raw)
Green Snap Beans
Sweet Potatoes
Peas
Beet Greens
Winter Squash
Onions (raw)

Vegetables—Vitamin A
Dandelion Greens (raw)
Carrots
Kale
Spinach
Winter Squash
Sweet Potatoes
Collards
Pumpkin
Turnip Greens
Mustard Greens
Beet Greens
Asparagus
Tomato Puree

*Fruits and vegetables are listed in order with the highest quantity given first.

Ascorbic Acid:

Make a solution of 1-1/2 tablespoons of ascorbic acid powder in 1 gallon of water. Dip fruit for 2 minutes, drain, and spread it on racks to dry. Ascorbic Acid is rather hard to buy, but markets have different trade-named products by the canning supplies and the frozen food counter that contain Ascorbic Acid.

Erythorbic Acid:

Dip fruit in a solution of 1 tablespoon of Erythorbic Acid and 1 gallon of water. Tests have been run on the length of time and it was found that 2 minutes is as effective as 3 minutes but is better than 1 minute.

Fruit Fresh:

This is a trade-name for Ascorbic Acid. To some people it is objectionable because it has sugar and a moisture inhibitor added. Use 3 tablespoons of water and 1 teaspoon of Fruit Fresh to start the solution. The juices from the fruit will build the amount. After treating approximately 10 pounds of fruit, add another teaspoon of Fruit Fresh.

Invert Sugars:

Dissolve 1/3 cup of honey in 1 cup of water. Coat fruit well, drain, and dehydrate.

Mix 1/2 cup of sugar, 1 cup water, 1/4 tablespoon of lemon juice. Place over heat and simmer for 25 to 30 minutes. Cool and dip fruit until well coated, drain, and dehydrate.

Combine 3/4 cup sugar, 1/4 cup light corn syrup, 1 teaspoon ascorbic acid powder, and 1 cup of warm water. Stir until sugar has completely dissolved. Cool, add cinnamon, nutmeg, etc., stir well, and dip (do not soak) fruit into mixture. Drip dry fruit slices. Place on netting and dehydrate. Spices are optional.

Pineapple Juice:

Dip fruits that would be enhanced by a pineapple flavor into the juice, drip dry, and dehydrate.

Sodium Bisulfite:

Use 1-1/2 tablespoons of sodium bisulfite dissolved in 1 gallon of water. Sodium bisulfite may be purchased at a chemical supply company. Do not confuse it with sodium sulfate known as Glauber's salt which is a cathartic and will cause diarrhea.

Steam Blanching:

Fruits may be placed in a colander or strainer in a double-boiler type of arrangement. Steam 5 minutes. Skins can be removed after blanching.

Sulfuring:

CAUTION: When sulfuring in a dehydrator, *do not use the trays purchased with the dehydrator* unless the manufacturer guarantees the tray to be safe when exposed to the burning sulfur fumes. Stainless steel mesh or wooden trays may be built to fit the dehydrator to be used when sulfuring. *Do not sulfur in the dehydrator*—a special sulfuring box must be built for this purpose.

After the fruit has been sulfured and placed in the dehydrator, *do not use the dehydrator in the house.* The fumes are irritating. It is best to use it outside where there is good circulation.

Sulfuring procedures, as previously given for sun drying, may be altered for dehydrator drying. Refer to Table 4 for reduced quantity and time requirements when using this pretreatment in a home dehydrator.

Water Blanching:

When water blanching, place the whole fruits in enough boiling water to cover them. Boil nectarines and peaches approximately 7 minutes and apricots 4 minutes. The fruits are cut and pitted after blanching. With either steam or water blanching, the skins may become loosened enough to be peeled off if desired.

Test Results of Vitamin C Preservation Methods

Tests show the following results with the various pretreatment procedures:

Table 4. SULFURING TABLE FOR FRUITS TO BE DRIED IN
THE DEHYDRATOR

FRUIT	AMOUNT OF SULFUR *	BURNING TIME
Apples	1 teaspoon of sulfur per pound of cut fruit	25 minutes
Apricots	1/2 teaspoon of sulfur per pound of cut fruit	1 hour
Nectarines	1 teaspoon of sulfur per pound of cut fruit	1-1/2 hours
Peaches	1 teaspoon of sulfur per pound of cut fruit	1-1/2 hours
Pears	1-1/4 teaspoons of sulfur per pound of cut fruit	2-1/2 hours

*With further experimentation it may be possible to reduce
the amount of sulfur even more.

Erythorbic Acid:

It is not recommended that this be used alone because it does
not maintain fruit color. A combination of this and Sodium Bisul
fite will treat with ascorbic acid and also maintain color.

Fruit Fresh:

This treats with ascorbic acid and maintains good color at
first, but the fruit loses its color during storage.

Invert Sugars:

The invert sugars have fair color and good flavor, but the
texture is not as good as sulfured fruit. The honey has the best
color, but no ascorbic acid is added in this solution.

Pineapple Juice:

This does not maintain good color, and the flavor is sometimes objectionable.

Sodium Bisulfite:

Fruits treated with this have good color and flavor. They have a higher retention of vitamin C. They seem to dry a little faster. Of course no ascorbic acid has been added so it would be better to mix this solution with the Erythorbic Acid solution and have the addition of vitamin C.

Steam Blanching:

The product is darker and has a slight cooked flavor. The fruits are soft and difficult to handle. Nutrition is lost in the blanching process. The texture is tough and chewy.

Sulfuring:

The fruit has a good texture. It is soft, pliable, retains more of the natural vitamin C, and has good color—even better than before it was sulfured (bruised spots are bleached). To some people the sulfur taste is objectionable.

Water Blanching:

The fruit is darker, has a cooked flavor, is soft and difficult to handle, and the peeled fruits may stick to the drying trays. More nutrition is lost by water blanching than by steam blanching. The finished product is tough and chewy.

CHAPTER VI

TWENTY-FIVE HELPFUL HINTS FOR THE DEHYDRATER

The secret of success in drying is a combination of things:

1. Start with mature top quality fruits and vegetables and prepare them properly.

2. It is important for warm air to circulate over the prepared food. The temperature should start at approximately 100° F. Never let the temperature go over 140° F. to help preserve nutrients. The ideal drying situation is recognized by touching the fruit or vegetable—the produce will feel cool, the air moving across it will be warm. When these conditions exist, evaporation is taking place.

3. Fruits and vegetables should be left in the dehydrator to cool, and then be placed directly into sterilized or scalded storage containers to eliminate the possibility of contamination.

4. Shake the storage bottle to stir the food each day for one week to make sure it has been dehydrated sufficiently. Remember to check the food about once a month to make sure it is not molding.

5. To have a good dried product, it is necessary to work fast for high vitamin content and better quality and flavor. It is not practical to dry foods that are not of top quality to begin with. Be familiar with produce characteristics with regard to cooking times. Italian beans cook faster than Kentucky Wonder, and this is important to know when steam blanching. Some carrots have a hard core which would not be advisable to use in dehydrating. The more uniform the slices of fruits and vegetables the more even the drying time.

6. Each one square foot of tray space will accommodate approximately 1-1/2 pounds of prepared food. Do not overcrowd trays. Slices should be placed close together, but only one layer deep to allow adequate air flow.

7. If more food is available than the dehydrator can accommodate, it can be placed in the refrigerator. It is not advisable to

keep it more than 24 hours. Corn should not be held over because it will change to starch.

8. Never prepare large amounts of food at one time. Fill one tray at a time, and place it into the dehydrator.

9. To prevent darkening of the produce when preparing food for the dehydrator, always use stainless steel or enamel strainers, steamers, knives, etc.

10. Do not leach vitamins and minerals from produce by soaking them in water when preparing them for dehydrating. Steam blanching is the best method for vegetables. Fruits should be coated with ascorbic acid and drained in a colander rather than to be soaked in water.

11. Nylon netting on trays will make sweet foods easier to remove when dry and will help hold vegetables that may drop through the regular tray mesh. Nylon netting may be washed in the washing machine, but do not let it go through the spin cycle or dry it in the dryer.

12. Maintain sanitary conditions when preparing food. Cleanliness is very important to assure a good end product. Scrub the dehydrator shelves with detergent after each use.

13. If the dryer is designed to use solar energy, it is important to observe the temperature closely. Do not let it go over 140° F. When it is cloudy or after sundown, it is necessary to turn on the heating element to maintain the desired temperature.

14. Foods with high moisture content have a very strong flavor when dried. Melon varieties dry beautifully but are so strongly flavored that they are disappointing to taste. Tomatoes are not a munching type food because of the strong flavor. However, they are excellent to use in cooking.

15. Strong smelling foods such as, beef jerky, fish, onion, etc. should not be dried with other foods. Do not place them directly on metal trays.

16. When experimenting, be sure to keep accurate written records of amounts, times, ingredients, etc. This is how successful

recipes are created. If a change is desired, it is easy to refer back to the original and make the improvement.

17.   Always label dehydrated foods. A lot of calories can be consumed trying to find a roll of apricot leather (by taste test) to make a chiffon pie.

18.   There are so many factors involved with drying times that it is difficult to give anything but an estimate. The size of the load, the thickness of the slices, the heat source, the humidity of the air, the moisture content of the food—all of these factors effect the drying time.

19.   Always let fruit, vegetables, meat, and fish cool before testing for dryness.

20.   Acid fruits should not be placed directly on metal trays for dehydration. Use nylon netting.

21.   Become familiar with "in season" times for produce to make economical and nutritional purchases.

22.   Kitchen shears make a handy tool for cutting and dicing dehydrated fruits for cookies, breads, yogurt, cereals, etc.

23.   Heat sealable cooking pouches are excellent for storing individual fruits in small quantities. The small bags must be stored in an insect-proof container to prevent bugs from chewing through the plastic. Many bags may be placed in a large plastic bucket without concern for flavor transfer when using the heat sealable bags.

24.   An excellent source for produce information useful in selecting foods for dehydrating is, *The Greengrocer*, by Joe Carcione and Bob Lucas, available from Pyramid Books.

25.   Dehydration knows "no season." To utilize a dehydrator during fall harvest is only partially taking advantage of the investment. Many products are available at lower cost during other seasons throughout the year. Pineapple, asparagus, bananas, strawberries and papaya are examples. Yogurt, granola, croutons, unbaked cookies, etc. make the dehydrator useful year round.

CHAPTER VII

FRUIT PREPARATION GUIDE

Preparing the Fruit

Most fruits and berries may be dried. Select fruit that is ripe or mature so that the sugar content is at its peak. If the fruits are dried with controlled heat and air, it is not necessary to sulfur them, but choose firm fruit. When humidity is low, it is possible to dry apricot halves that look beautiful, but with high humidity they do not look as eye appealing. Pretreated fruits will retain more vitamin C and more of their natural color than untreated fruits.

When using a solar drier, it is necessary to pretreat the fruit. Sun shining directly on fruits (such as apricots, peaches, pears, and apples) causes oxidation to take place. Oxidation turns the fruit dark. Acid retards the enzyme action. (See Chapter V.)

Checking

By peeling apples, pears, and peaches the flavor and especially the appearance is improved. The drying time is also reduced. It is not necessary to peel apricots or nectarines. Tough-skinned fruits such as plums, figs, blueberries, or grapes require a process called checking. It is necessary to craze the protective wax coating of the skin to allow the internal moisture to come to the surface to be evaporated. Dip the fruits or berries into briskly boiling water for from 30 to 60 seconds, then place them in ice water and drain. The length of the dip depends on how tough the fruits' skins are. Place them on absorbent toweling to remove the excess moisture and then put on trays to dry. This procedure reduces the drying time.

To prepare fruit for drying, sort and discard defective fruits. Wash thoroughly, pit stone fruits, check skins on those fruits to be dried whole (such as grapes, blueberries, etc.), scald tomatoes to remove skins, and peel other fruits. Most recipes call for pieces of fruit. Fruits that are cut into 1/4-inch to 3/8-inch pieces not only dry faster but also reconstitute faster. With experience comes knowledge as to what size is preferred for various recipes. Diced apples, peaches, etc. are excellent in yogurt, milk shakes, ice cream, and granola. When slices are approximately the same thickness, the fruit drys more evenly. It is not necessary to measure each slice. Because of the sugar content fruits have a tendency to stick to the dryer trays. To prevent this it is wise to use nylon netting.

If a vegetable spray (such as Pam) is to be used, be sure to wash the trays thoroughly after each use. When they have been exposed to the heat of the dryer, the spray build-up will turn the tray black.

After the fruit is sliced, dip it immediately into the chosen pretreatment solution. Remove it from the solution and place it into a colander to drip dry. The slices should then be placed close together on the tray (only one layer deep to allow for air circulation and more efficient drying), and put into the preheated dryer. Prepare only one tray at a time. Speed helps preserve color.

With cherries place the skin side on the net with the center facing up. With fruits that are quartered, place the skin side on the net. As the moisture evaporates, the nutrients will fall into the hollow part of the quarter-moon shape instead of dripping onto the tray to be lost.

Pretreatment of Skins for Easy Removal

Caustic soda or lye has been suggested by some for use in removing the skins of cling peaches, pears, nectarines, etc., and to check skins of firm fruits and berries that have a wax coating such as plums, grapes, huckleberries, etc. The alkali in soda compounds is detrimental to some B vitamins and vitamin C. Is the use of such a harsh chemical wise?

CAUTION: Lye attacks most metals and can cause serious burns to the body. Use rubber gloves when handling it. If lye contacts the skin, wash immediately with water.

Stainless steel, earthenware or enamelware (if it has no chips or cracks) are safe containers to use with lye. Use only stainless steel colanders and wooden spoons when working with lye.

Berries and firm fruits may have the skins checked by immersing them in boiling water for 30 to 60 seconds. Peaches may be scalded to remove their skins. Nectarines do not require removal of their skins, but pears are better peeled.

For individuals that prefer the lye solution, they may obtain more information with regard to procedure, amounts, disposal, etc. by contacting the county home agent from their area.

Dehydrofreezing

The dehydrofreezing of fruits is a new process—a combination of drying and freezing. About half of the water is evaporated out, then the food is bagged and placed in the deepfreeze. The more moisture that is left in the fruit, the more tender the fruit will be when it is reconstituted. However, the storage life will be shorter when the fruit is thawed, and it should be stored in the refrigerator.

Sulfuring for the Dehydrator

For those people desiring to sulfur their fruit outside and dry it in the dehydrator, the following guidelines may prove beneficial.

Sulfur dioxide fumes penetrate the fruit when sulfur is burned. This penetration affects the fruit in the following ways:

1. It increases the permeability of the flesh, causing the fruit to dry faster without air-pockets.

2. It bleaches the fruit and the color remains bright. Over-ripe fruit that would be mushy if wet-packed can be sulfured and dried. The sulfuring process removes browned areas caused from bruises. Sulfur inactivates the enzymes, thus preventing further deterioration by oxidation. This does not mean that moldy fruit or fruit with rotten spots can be used—just extra-ripe sound fruit.

3. It acts as a preservative and insect repellant while the fruit is drying and airing.

4. The drying process may be stopped while the fruit is soft and pliable. The color is good, it retains its original shape, and the vitamin C content is high. People with sensitive tastebuds may find the sulfur taste objectionable.

5. Refer to Chapter 2 for information about safe sulfuring materials, trays, the sulfuring box and its use, the kind of sulfur, etc.

6. See Table 4 with regard to sulfuring times and amounts required when using a home dehydrator.

7. After the sulfur has burned, remove the cardboard box, place the net trays into the dehydrator, place the dehydrator in the garage or on the patio, turn on the fan and the heater and dry away, checking occasionally to see if the fruit needs to be rotated. When the fruit is soft, pliable, and slightly moist in the center, it

should be removed from the dehydrator. The fruit must then be placed into an enameled pan or crock to air (let the sulfur fumes dissipate). Place muslin over the top of the pan to prevent insect infestation. Stir the fruit each day to allow unexposed fruit to be exposed to the air. After about one week, check the fruit for sulfur taste. When it is ready to package, place it in plastic bags (if it is to be packaged in metal containers), or in plastic bottles. Place a double layer of plastic wrap over the mouth of the jar to prevent sulfur fumes from coming into contact with the metal from the lid. If there is any possibility that the fruit may have been contaminated while it was conditioning, it is wise to place the fruit and storage containers into the deepfreeze at 0° F. for 48 hours to kill any insect eggs on the fruit. The fruit may then be stored on the shelf in a dry, cool, dark place.

Drying Times

There are so many variables involved in drying times that exact drying times are little more than guesswork. All fruits will be dry in from 10 hours to 36 hours. One week it may take 12 hours to dry peach slices. If it is rainy the following week, it may take 24 hours before they are completely dry. The drying process is one that cannot be rushed. The size, pretreatment, humidity, moisture content of the fruit, and how heavily loaded the trays are—these are all determining factors in the speed of drying.

When purchasing fruit in quantity for dehydration, use caution in the amounts purchased. Know the capacity of the dehydrator in pounds. Consider the moisture content of the fruit, the ripeness of the fruit, the relative humidity of the air, and the temperature. With this knowledge, it will be easy to determine the amount of fruit to purchase.

Table 5. AVERAGE DRYING TIME FOR FRUITS

PRODUCT	SIZE	HOURS
Apples	Slices	12 to 15
Apricots	Halves	24 to 36
Bananas	Slices	15 to 24
Berries	Whole Except Strawberries	12 to 24
Cherries	Whole, pitted	20 to 36
Figs	Quarters	12 to 20
Grapes	Whole (Checked)	12 to 20
Nectarines	Slices	12 to 24
Pears	Slices	15 to 24
Peaches	Slices	12 to 24
Plums	Quarters	12 to 20
Prunes	Whole (Checked)	24 to 36
Rhubarb	Slices	12 to 15

This table is only a general guideline for approximate drying times.

CHAPTER VIII

HERB PREPARATION GUIDE

Gathering and Preparing Herbs

To know and understand the uses of herbs is a study in and of itself. There are many books available discussing uses, ways of preserving, and how to gather herbs. This chapter deals with a few of the more common herbs found in the kitchen.

When gathering herbs, be careful not to get dead leaves, other plants, etc. Precaution saves preparation time before drying. Never heat herbs over 100-105° F. They lose the oils that give them flavor. Do not dry herbs in direct sunlight, or expose them to light, because they will lose color.

If the dehydrator has a switch to turn off the heating element, or a thermostat that can be set, make sure the temperature does not go over 100-105° F. With some models the fan is all that is required for drying herbs.

Storage of Herbs

Store leaves of herbs whole. They retain more flavor whole, and can be ground or rubbed just before using. An example would be sage. Just rub the whole leaves in the palm of the hand, and make a powder to be used in the recipe.

To store leaves, seeds, or roots, put them into a lightly sealed jar in a warm place for one week. At the end of a week, check the jars for moisture content. If moisture beads up on the inside of the glass or on the lid, put the contents back into the dryer and dry them longer. This will prevent mold from forming. Herbs should be stored in a cool, dry, dark place. Aluminum foil or black plastic will keep out the light if brown jars are not available.

Do not store herbs in paper bags. The paper absorbs the oil from the leaves and they lose their flavor. Be sure to mark the contents and date on all packages or jars. Some herbs are hard to identify after storage.

It is not necessary to powder herbs for tea. Use 1 heaping teaspoonful of dried herb, and 1 cup of boiling water. Steep for 5 minutes (longer if a stronger flavored tea is desired), strain through a tea strainer, add honey or lemon juice if desired, and enjoy it.

CHAPTER IX

MEAT AND FISH PREPARATION GUIDE

There are two ways to preserve meat by dehydration. The most popular is to make jerked beef. The second way is to precook meat to the tender-done stage and then dehydrate it in cubes or slices to be used in main dishes for convenience foods, camping, and backpacking.

If meat is prepared in cubes or slices for rehydration in soups, stroganoff, etc., it should be precooked to the tender-done stage and stored at 40° F. or below. Fat becomes rancid if stored above refrigerator temperatures.

Temperature

The temperature range for dehydrating meats and fish should be 140° F. to 150° F. If nonacid meat and fish are left at temperatures from 40° F. to 140° F. growth cells of micro-organisms begin to be active. At 140° F. the growth cells are killed, but the spores still live. That is why it is important to not let the spoilers get started. To prevent their growth the meat and fish should be dried at a temperature above 140° F., but not over 150° F., or the meat will taste cooked. This does not apply to the precooked meat previously mentioned.

Fish

There are as many variations in drying fish as there are in making jerky. Large fish should be cut into smaller pieces or dry cured. Small fish may be dried whole. There are two basic ways of preparing fish before they are dehydrated—by dry curing or brine curing. Instructions and recipes are available in the recipe section.

Jerked Meat

The process of cutting meat into long strips and drying it in the sun is known as jerking beef. Of course other meats may also be used to make jerky. Precautions must be taken to make sure that game meat is cooled rapidly and carefully handled to keep it clean, thereby avoiding contamination and possible food poisoning from improper handling.

Jerky is a seasoned meat that remains tough and leathery and is eaten as a snack food. Marinades may be varied according to individual taste. The recipe section contains directions and seasonings for making jerky. Be sure to remove any beads of oil with paper toweling that may be on the strips of jerky before placing it into storage.

Because raw pork may contain trichinae, it is not wise to use it for jerky. To make jerked ham, use fully cooked, boneless ham sliced in long strips 1/8-inch to 1/4-inch thick. Ham does not need to be marinated because it has already been seasoned.

CHAPTER X

VEGETABLE PREPARATION GUIDE

Vegetable Selection

If vegetables aren't in prime condition, they will not be appetizing after they are dehydrated. Because they are low-acid, vegetables have to be handled more carefully to prevent spoilage while drying. Vegetables dried in controlled heat are more appetizing than sun-dried vegetables. They also have a higher vitamin A content with better color and flavor.

Vegetables should be picked fresh and not allowed to stand at room temperature. Deterioration has already begun in wilted vegetables. Steam blanching vegetables speeds up the drying time by softening the tissues, setting the color, stopping the ripening process, and preventing undesirable flavor changes during the dehydration process.

Vegetables should be washed thoroughly to remove dust and insecticides. Inferior vegetables should be discarded. Handle the food carefully, and keep it clean. Work quickly. Cut or break vegetables into 1/4-inch to 3/8-inch pieces or grate them. Prepare food for one tray at a time and place it promptly into the preheated dehydrator.

Blanching

Vegetables that are steam blanched before drying do not require as long a soaking time before they are cooked. Most vegetables should be blanched. There are a few exceptions which will be mentioned under the specific vegetables in the recipe section.

Blanching is the process of heating vegetables to a temperature high enough to inactivate enzymes so they will not cause deterioration of the food during drying and storage. Steam blanching is preferred to water blanching because many vitamins and minerals are water soluble and will be leached out in the blanching process. Under-blanching will produce an inferior product because enzyme action was not inactivated; however, over-blanching will result in an inferior product that has lost water soluble vitamins and minerals and become unappetizing.

To steam blanch, choose a pan (with a tight-fitting lid) larger than the colander, wire basket, or sieve to be used to hold the vegetables (stainless steel or enameled colander). Put two inches of boiling water in the bottom of the pan. Set the steamer or colander on a rack above the water. Do not let the water touch the vegetables. Put a shallow layer of vegetables in the steamer, cover the pan tightly with the lid, and keep the water boiling rapidly. Heat until all vegetables in the steamer are tender or translucent. Test by cutting through the center of the vegetable to see if it is cooked almost to the center. Cool rapidly in ice water to stop the cooking process. Drain in the colander for one minute so the excess water runs off. Place the vegetables on a clean terry towel or absorbent paper toweling to absorb the remaining moisture before putting them into the dehydrator.

After the moist food is placed in the preheated dehydrator, the temperature will drop to around 100° F.; but as the warm air circulates over the food and moves out of the dehydrator vents, the temperature will gradually rise. Examine the vegetables from time to time to see if rotation is necessary. Close to the end of the drying time, it is necessary to watch for scorching. Scorch should be avoided because it is noticeable in the finished product. The amount of drying time required varies with the size of pieces, moisture content of the food, humidity in the air, etc.

Storage

Let the vegetables remain in the dehydrator with just the fan turned on until they are cool. Pack immediately into the storage containers to prevent contamination.

Table 6. STEAMING TIME—AVERAGE DRYING TIMES FOR
         VEGETABLES

Vegetable	Steaming Time	Drying Time
Asparagus	4-5 minutes	9 hours
Beans, Green	5 minutes	12-14 hours
Beans, Italian	1 minute	12-14 hours
Beets, small	Cook	10-12 hours
Carrots	5 minutes	10-12 hours
Carrots (grated)	None	8-10 hours
Celery	None	12-14 hours
Corn	5 minutes or until milk is set	12-15 hours
Cucumber	Optional 2 minutes	12-14 hours
Eggplant	4 minutes	12-14 hours
Mushrooms	None	8-10 hours
Onions	None	8-10 hours
Peas	2 minutes	8-10 hours
Peppers, Bell	None	8-12 hours
Peppers, Hot	None, dry whole	8-12 hours
Potatoes	5 minutes	8-12 hours
Squash, Summer	Optional 2 minutes	10-12 hours
Squash, Winter	3 minutes	10-16 hours
Sweet Potatoes	4 minutes	10-16 hours
Tomatoes	None	10-19 hours

Note: Cool the test piece of vegetable before testing for dryness.

The above table lists only approximate steaming times and drying times. As mentioned previously, the variables are too great to give an exact time. Refer to the recipe section for more detailed information concerning the preparation of each individual vegetable.

CHAPTER XI

TESTING FOR DRYNESS

Fish

Remove a piece of fish from the dehydrator and let it cool before testing. The fish will have a brown satiny texture when it is done. It will be firm and hard with no soft spots.

Fruits

Remove a piece of fruit from the dehydrator, let it cool, and break it open. If moisture beads up on the broken sides, it is not sufficiently dry to avoid spoilage. If the fruit is to be kept for long time storage, return it to the dehydrator for more processing. A small amount of moisture will require refrigerator storage for snack foods, and deepfreeze storage if the fruit is to be preserved by dehydrofreezing.

Jerky

Jerky will be leathery when it is dry. It will not break just by bending it, but it will crack. Force must be used to break off a piece. It is important to keep jerky in an airtight container in a cool, dark place. For long time storage it should be refrigerated or kept in the freezer.

Meats

All of the meats, turkey, chicken, beef, etc., will be crisp when they are sufficiently dried for storage. Be sure all of the fat is removed to avoid the unpleasant taste of rancid fat when it is taken out of refrigeration for use. These meats may be used as snack foods, but because they were precooked, it is possible to rehydrate them for use in camping.

Vegetables

Vegetables will be tough or brittle when they are dry. Vegetables such as peas and corn will rattle on the trays. Carrots, squash and peppers will be tough like a piece of leather.

Fruits and vegetables fall into one of three categories. They are leathery, pliable, or brittle (rattles). The following table will place them in the category into which they most appropriately fit. With experience comes the ability to "feel" whether or not the fruits, meats, and vegetables are sufficiently dry for the type of storage desired.

Table 7. TESTS FOR DRYNESS

Leathery	Pliable	Brittle (rattles)
Apples	Apricots	Rhubarb
Bananas	Nectarines	Asparagus
Berries	Peaches	Beans
(almost rattles	Large Plums	Carrots (grated)
Beets	Prunes	Celery
Carrots	Cherries	Corn
Cucumber	Figs	Peas
Eggplant	Grapes	Potatoes
Mushrooms	Pears	Sweet Potatoes
Onions	Tomatoes	
Winter Squash		
Summer Squash		
(almost rattles)		

Note: Remember to cool the pieces of food before testing for dryness.

CHAPTER XII

LABELING, PACKAGING & STORAGE

Labeling

It is very important to label dried foods. It is also wise to include the date they were dehydrated. This enables the food dated earliest to be used first. The longer the food is in storage the more nutrition is lost; therefore, use good organization in storing and using dehydrated foods. A proper label eliminates guesswork with regard to types of herbs, leathers, etc.

Packaging

Insectproof packaging materials are necessary. When dehydrated foods are removed from the dryer, they are free from infestation. They should be packaged as soon as they are cool; otherwise, they are susceptible to contamination. They should be placed in clean containers that are free from moisture and insectproof.

Glass jars with well-fitting lids, plastic bottles (discards salvaged from restaurants, school lunch, or hospitals), and plastic heat sealable cooking pouches (when placed in insect safe outer containers) are excellent. Number 10 metal cans or shortening cans may be used if they have been dried thoroughly, and the food is placed in a plastic bag first.

If dehydrated food is appetizing to people, it will also be appetizing to insects. It is necessary to package the food in a manner that prevents infestation. Insects can chew through freezer bags so it necessitates storage in the freezer, plastic buckets, or metal cans if freezer bags are to be used. When storing in glass jars (if they are not stored in a dark place), it will be necessary to cover the outside of the bottle with black plastic or foil.

The food should be packed into the container as compactly as possible without crushing. To avoid contamination of bulk supplies, transfer food for daily use into smaller containers.

Storage

Storage conditions for dehydrated foods are improved when air, light, moisture, and heat are kept at a minimum.

Lower storage temperatures help extend the shelf life of dried food, and help maintain color, flavor, and quality. As a general rule plan only for ten to twelve month storage. Some foods deteriorate more rapidly than others. It is not necessary to store dried food in the freezer, but if the space is available, vitamin loss is reduced. Freezer space is usually at a premium. With the reduction of bulk through dehydration, it is possible to store larger quantities of food in a freezer than would be otherwise possible.

For long-time storage of snack foods (containing more moisture), an old refrigerator kept at "vacation" temperature is ideal.

CHAPTER XIII

REHYDRATION

Time To Put It Back Again—Water That Is!

Water-soluble nutrients distribute themselves evenly throughout the solids and liquids. If too much water is added when reconstituting dehydrated food, nutritional loss is evident. If the solids constitute two-thirds of the total, one-third of the water-soluble nutrients will be lost if the liquid is not used.

The amount of water dried food will absorb and the time it takes for complete rehydration varies according to the size of the food and its degree of dryness. If the water is absorbed quickly and the food looks shriveled, add a little more water until the food will hold no more.

Directions for Fruits

Most fruits will not be rehydrated but eaten dried. When using fruit in recipes for pies, cobblers, and other similar types of dessert, the general rule is to add 1 cup of fruit to 1 cup of boiling water. Let it rehydrate for 5 minutes, and then proceed with the recipe. When using fruit in yogurt it is not necessary to add additional water. To use the fruit concentrated for ice cream, shakes, etc., just add 3/4 cup of boiling water, let it stand for 5 minutes to soften, and it is ready to be used in the recipe.

If after long storage time, the fruit is more firm than desired (too chewy), "tenderize" it by placing it into boiling water for 15 seconds. Let it drip dry on paper towels. If it isn't used immediately, it would be wise to store it in the refrigerator to prevent molding.

Directions for Meat

Jerky, of course, is not rehydrated. Fish is not rehydrated. Meat may be used as snack foods, or rehydrated for use in meat pies, etc. Use cup for cup of meat and water to rehydrate for meat pies, stroganoff, etc. Place the meat in boiling water and let it stand for 5 minutes, and then cook with it. Bring it to a boil, reduce the heat, and let it simmer until it is tender.

Directions for Vegetables

The general rule for rehydrating vegetables is to add 1-1/2 cups of boiling water to each cup of vegetable. Allow them to stand for 5 minutes and they are ready to prepare. The advantage in using dehydrated vegetables is the fact that they taste like fresh-picked produce.

Powdered dehydrated vegetables do not need to be reconstituted when they are used as seasonings for salads, casseroles, etc. One tablespoon of dehydrated tomatoes reconstituted with 1/2 cup of boiling water makes a convenient tomato sauce.

After rehydration, simmer the vegetable for 10 minutes or until it is tender, then season and serve it. Some vegetables and fruits may be reconstituted in the liquid required in the recipe. An example is pineapple juice used as the moisture for sweet potatoes in a candied casserole.

There are so many discrepancies concerning the rehydration of fruits and vegetables that experiments were performed by the author. Corn and apples were rehydrated as follows:

1/4 cup corn + 3/8 cup of boiling water soaking 5 minutes.
1/4 cup corn + 3/8 cup of boiling water soaking 30 minutes.
1/4 cup corn + 3/8 cup of boiling water soaking 90 minutes.
1/4 cup corn + 3/8 cup of boiling water soaking overnight.

The second test was run with the same amounts of corn, water, and soaking times; but salt was added to the boiling water as a seasoning at the time of rehydration.

The result: No more water was absorbed by the corn that soaked overnight than the corn that soaked 5 minutes. The exception was the salted water test. The second test group, where salt had been added, did not absorb as much of the water: 1/8 of a cup of water was left after the time lapse. This indicates that it is best to season the vegetables after the initial rehydration step. It also shows that it is not necessary to risk the chance of microorganism growth by letting the food stand for hours since the same amount of moisture is absorbed in 5 minutes.

All batches of corn cooked in 10 minutes time, but the corn with salt added at the beginning of rehydration was a little more chewy than the corn that was seasoned after rehydration.

In the apple experiment, the same amount of apples, water, and soaking times were used. The second test had sugar added instead of the salt which was added to the corn.

The results were the same. When sugar is added at the beginning of rehydration, the fruit does not absorb as much of the water. There is no reason to soak the fruit overnight when the same amount of water is absorbed in 5 minutes. Because of the natural sweetness in dehydrated fruits, it is not necessary to add the full amount of sugar called for in recipes using fresh fruit.

CHAPTER XIV

BUY IT   DRY IT   TRY IT
GUIDE

APPLES

*Gravenstein, Jonathan, Rome Beauty and Golden Delicious
are good varieties for dehydrating.*

Buy apples by variety, and in bushel quantities for best buys.
Apples that have both a red color and a background color (green
then yellow) like the Jonathan should be purchased more red
than green. The red side of a well-colored apple will contain more
vitamin C, and more sugar than the green half of the same fruit.
The apples should be free of bruises, stem-punctures, and insect
stings. An exception to this rule is when the fruit is to be used for
making fruit leather. This is where imperfect fruit may be used.
The Golden Delicious and the Gravenstein apples do not turn
brown as readily as other varieties when sliced. Apples are best
stored at 60° F. Summer apples come to market in June, July,
and August. Winter apples are available from October through
December.

Prepare: Wash fruit thoroughly. Pare, core, and remove any blem-
ish. Slice in 3/8-inch slices or 3/8-inch rings. Pretreat with ascorbic
acid. Drain in colander. Place on a dryer tray covered with nylon
netting and dry. Some apples should be diced for use in granola,
fruit desserts, and breads.

Apple slices may be dipped into a mixture of ascorbic acid
that has cinnamon or nutmeg added to it. This distributes the
spice evenly and makes a good snack. It is not effective to just
sprinkle spices over the pieces—some get too much and some get
too little.

Apple Pudding

Use 4 cups apple slices reconstituted in 3-1/2 cups of boiling
water. Stir occasionally so all apples will have an opportunity to
rehydrate. Let them stand 5 minutes, or until the moisture is

almost absorbed (1/2 cup juice is sufficient). Spread into a 9 x 13-inch oblong baking pan. Sprinkle with 1/2 cup of granulated sugar and 1 teaspoon of cinnamon.

In a separate bowl, mix with a fork until crumbly:

1 cup flour	1 tsp baking powder
1 cup sugar	1/2 tsp salt
1 tsp nutmeg	1 egg slightly beaten

When it is very crumbly, sprinkle it over the top of the apples. Bake at 400° F. for 30 minutes, or until the apples are tender and the crust is browned.

For variety, add 1/2 cup crunchy (nut variety) granola to the above mixture before baking.

No-Crust Dutch Apple Pie

Use 2 cups apple slices reconstituted in 1-3/4 cups of boiling water. Let them stand until the water is almost absorbed and the apples are plump. Place them in a deep-dish pie plate. Sprinkle 2 tablespoons of granulated sugar and 1 teaspoon of cinnamon over the top.

In a separate bowl, mix the following ingredients:

1 cup brown sugar	1/2 square margarine
1 cup flour	1/2 tsp salt

Stir the above mixture with a fork until it is crumbly. Spread it over the top of the apples, and bake at 400° F. for 30 minutes.

APRICOTS

Royal, Blenheim, and Tilton are good varieties for dehydrating. They are usually all marketed under the trade name of Royal.

Apricots do not ripen after picking. They must be picked mature and sweet. They should look plump and juicy and have a golden-yellow background color and red blushed cheeks. Avoid shriveled, dull-looking, or firm, pale yellow or greenish-yellow colored cots. The fruit will color up and soften, but it will not be as flavorful because it was picked too green. Any bruised fruit should be used for leather. Choose only firm apricots for dehydrating. Apricots are available in June and July.

Prepare: Wash carefully, remove pit, pretreat with ascorbic acid, drain in colander, place on a net on trays, and dry. Depending on the use for the fruit, cut it into halves, quarters, dices, or slices for use in granola, desserts, and breads. Spices may be added to the ascorbic acid for coating apricots for variety snacks.

Caution: When drying apricot halves, be careful not to overload the dehydrator. If too many cot halves are placed on each tray, they may mold before the heating element and fan can move the moisture away. One pound of apricot halves per 12 x 12-inch tray is ample for good drying conditions. If the weather is humid, that may even be too much fruit per tray.

While an apricot half is drying, the juice accumulates in the hollow of the half. To speed drying time, the skin side of the cot can be pushed up with thumbs causing an arch the opposite direction of the hollow. However, when this is done, the juice then drips onto the tray and good nutrients are lost. It is better to cut the cot in smaller pieces, thereby exposing more of the surface to warm air for rapid evaporation, than to lose the nutritious juices.

Apricots and Curried Meat Balls

1 pound ground beef	1 tsp curry powder
1 tsp salt	1 tsp honey or sugar
1/8 tsp pepper	2 cups beef broth
3 Tbsp vegetable oil	1 cup dried apricots (slices)
1 cup finely chopped,	1 Tbsp cornstarch
peeled onion	3 cups cooked rice

Mix beef with salt and pepper, and shape into 16 one-inch meat balls. Brown the meat balls in 2 tablespoons of the oil over moderate heat. Remove browned meat balls. Add the remaining tablespoon of oil, the onion, and brown. Add the curry powder and cook, stirring constantly, about 2 minutes. Stir in the honey, 1-3/4 cups broth, apricots, meat balls, and bring to a boil; turn heat down, cover pan and simmer 15 minutes. Mix cornstarch with the other 1/4 cup broth. Stir sauce in skillet and cook, stirring constantly, a few seconds. Serve curried meat balls with hot, cooked rice. Brown or white rice may be used according to individual taste. Makes 4 servings.

Apricot Penuche

1 cup granulated sugar	1 tsp vanilla
1-1/2 cups light brown	1/3 cup finely chopped
sugar, packed	dried apricots
1/3 cup condensed milk	1/3 cup finely chopped
1/3 cup milk	almonds
2 Tbsp margarine	

Butter an 8 x 8-inch pan; set aside. In a 2 quart pan combine sugars, cream, milk, and margarine; stir until it is well combined. Cook over medium heat, stirring constantly, until sugars dissolve and mixture begins to boil. Cook until mixture reaches 238° F. on candy thermometer. Remove pan from heat; cool mixture to 110° F. without stirring. Add vanilla to cooled mixture. Beat vigorously until candy thickens and starts to lose its gloss. Quickly stir in the apricots and nuts; spread evenly in the pan. Cool; cut when cool and firm. Serve.

ASPARAGUS

Martha or Mary Washington are good varieties.

The part of the asparagus stalk that has never been exposed to the sun will be white. Look for firm, straight stalks, with tips that are well-formed and tightly closed. Avoid limp, wilted stalks. Asparagus should be used as soon as possible after harvesting. April and May are peak harvest months.

Prepare: Rinse the stalks in cold, running water to eliminate sand or grit. Snap off (at the place where it will break easily), and discard tough, woody parts of each stalk. It is difficult to identify tender asparagus if it is cut with a knife—the break test is best for tender asparagus. Steam blanch for 5 minutes, or until tender. Do not over blanch or the asparagus will be mushy when it is rehydrated. Break it into 3/4-inch pieces. After blanching, put it into cold water to stop the cooking process. Drain on a terry towel. Place on a net-covered tray in the dehydrator.

Asparagus Soup

3 cups dehydrated asparagus	4 Tbsp butter or margarine
reconstituted in	4 Tbsp flour
4-1/2 cups water	1-1/4 tsp salt
milk	1/4 tsp white pepper

Cover asparagus with boiling water and let it simmer until it is tender. Puree asparagus with cooking liquid in an electric blender. Strain puree through a fine strainer, and discard fibrous part. There should be about 3-3/4 cups of thin puree. Add enough milk to make 4 cups.

In a medium saucepan melt butter, and stir in the flour until it is well-blended. Gradually stir in the asparagus puree. Cook over moderately low heat, stirring constantly, until it is thickened. Season with salt and pepper. Add a little more milk or cream, if desired. Makes about 1 quart.

AVOCADOS

Because of oil content (approximately 16 percent) avocados are not recommended for dehydrating.

BANANAS

Cavendish and Gros Michel bananas are sold by the importers' brand name—"Chiquita" and "Dole."

When a banana is solid yellow with specks of brown, it is in prime eating condition. The speckled banana has the lowest starch (it drops from 20 percent to 1 percent) and the highest sugar (it increases from 1 percent to 15 percent) as it ripens to the speckled brown stage.

Bananas should be held at room temperature until they are fully ripe and then they may be kept in the refrigerator. When the produce manager finds his bananas ripening too rapidly and offers them as trimmer bananas at reduced prices—that is the time to buy. Those with brown skins may be used to make banana leather and the speckled ones cut for use in cereal, granola, breads, and snack chips or sticks. They are available year round.

Prepare: Cut bananas in 1/4-inch slices, cubes, or sticks (cut the banana in half lengthwise and then into eighths). Dip into a lemon juice and honey mixture, or into ascorbic acid. Use 1/4 cup of honey, 1 tablespoon of lemon juice and enough water to make a manageable syrup (no more than 1/4 cup).

It is not necessary to pretreat bananas, unless a lighter color is preferred. One cup of banana slices and 1-1/2 cups of water reconstituted, equal 2 cups of banana. Let the banana stand for

5 minutes and then mash. It is ready to be used in banana bread, cake, waffles, etc.

GREEN SNAP BEANS

Kentucky Wonder, Improved Kentucky Wonder, Blue Lake, and Italian are varieties that can be dehydrated.

Look for good-colored pods with small beans. Beans that have been harvested with a mechanical harvester are sometimes snapped off below the stem. Avoid harvester-damaged beans because they will sour easily. Beans are available abundantly from July through September.

Prepare: Wash, snap off stem ends, remove any loose strings, cut into 3/4-inch pieces so they will dry fast. Care must be exercised with beans to prevent flat-sour. Steam blanch the beans until they are translucent or tender. Italian beans need only to be blanched for 2 or 3 minutes, while Wonder and Blue Lake need a 10 to 15 minute blanching time. After they reach the tender stage, plunge them immediately into ice water to stop the cooking process. Place on an absorbent towel to remove excess water and then place on nylon netting on dehydrator trays. They are dry when they are brittle and rattle.

Green Beans and Bacon

2 cups dehydrated beans
   reconstituted in
3 cups of boiling water
   (Cook for about 10
   minutes until tender.)
2 slices of bacon, cooked
   and crumbled
1 can Cream of Chicken Soup
   (Do not add water.)

1 can Cream of Mushroom
   Soup (Do not add water.)
1 cup grated cheese
1/2 tsp salt
pepper to taste
1 tsp Worcestershire sauce

Simmer beans for about 10 minutes until all of the water has been absorbed. Add condensed soup, salt, pepper, and Worcestershire sauce. Spread into a 9 x 13-inch oblong pan. If mixture is too thick to spread easily, a little water may be added. Sprinkle with cheese and crumbled bacon. Heat in a 350° F. oven for 20 minutes. Cover the top with frozen onion rings and increase the temperature to 400° F. and heat for 5 minutes or until browned. Serve.

BEETS

Detroit Dark Red and Early Wonder are good varieties.

Choose small, young, tender beets. The larger beets are woody and tough. Beets are harvested from June through October. In some areas beets are planted in a winter-garden. If beets can be grown year round, it is not necessary to dehydrate them.

Prepare: Do not cut the beet before cooking or all of the red pigment will be lost. Leave 1/2-inch of the tops on the beet. Scrub them thoroughly with a vegetable brush. Steam blanch until they are tender, cool in cold water, peel, cut in 1/4-inch cubes or circles and place on the dehydrator trays to dehydrate.

Beets in Orange Sauce

2 cups diced beets reconstituted in	3 cups of water (boiling) (Let simmer until tender.)

Mix together and stir in:

3 Tbsp flour	1 cup orange juice
1/4 cup sugar	2 Tbsp butter

Cook, stirring constantly until smoothly blended and thickened.

BERRIES

Berries are grouped into two types—the firm berry with the protective wax coating, and the soft berry that has to be handled very carefully.

Rather than to discuss each berry individually, it will be best to give directions for one and the others from the group should be processed in the same manner. Raspberries and strawberries will be discussed separately.

All berries are delicate and must be handled with care. Avoid cups with stained bottoms—a sign of overripe fruit. Berries are in season from May through August, with the biggest supply available during June and August.

Blackberries, Dewberries—Avoid fruit with red and black drupelets because they will have poor flavor.

Boysenberries—They are large, long, and dark reddish-black when fully ripe.

Loganberries—They are large, long, and dark-red when ripe.

Olallieberries—(A cross between a youngberry and a black loganberry.) They are bright black and medium sized when ripe.

Youngberries—They are large, sweet, and wine-colored when they are ripe.

Berries may be used in shakes, ice cream, yogurt, cereals, muffins, granola, pies, etc.

Prepare: To dry whole, soft berries, sort, wash carefully and place on nylon netting on trays to dry.

If seeds prove objectionable, the berries can be pureed for fruit leather; however, the use is limited to shakes, ice cream, etc. Leather wouldn't be used in cereals, muffins, yogurt, etc. Place the fruit in the blender and puree it. Strain the seeds and place on plastic wrap to dry. To reconstitute the leather for use in malts, syrups, etc; use 1 cup of the broken pieces of leather, 3/4 cup of water and let it reconstitute for 10 minutes. Blend until well-mixed, and use to make pancake syrup, malt, etc.

When a juicer is used to make the leather, sometimes the juice is so thin that it is hard to keep it on the plastic wrap to dry. The solution to this problem is to add apple, Arrowroot Powder, Karaya Gum Powder, or Keltone. These act as thickening agents. The natural pectin in apples will gel the juicy berries, but be careful not to use too much apple and lose the berry flavor.

Cranberries—There is a choice between the large bright-red tart type and the small dark-colored cranberry which is usually sweeter. Look for fresh, plump berries. Avoid shriveled, dull-looking berries.

Currants—Currants are not as sweet as raisins but are called for in combination with raisins in cookies, fruit cakes and boiled puddings.

Gooseberries—They are very good combined with sweet berries in leather—gooseberry/strawberry. They are good in tarts. Use ripened gooseberries to make tarts (they turn pink on the bush).

Huckleberries—They contain large boney seeds and are not as good as other varieties unless the seeds are strained out.

Blueberries—Some varieties are Earliblue (early) and Berkeley (late mid-season). They are all large, light blue in color and quite firm. Wildberries are usually more tart and not as large as the commercial varieties. Blueberries bruise easily. They should be poured rather than handled individually after picking. Look for fresh, plump berries. Plan to use them the same day they are purchased. If an emergency arises, then store the berries in the refrigerator. Overripe berries will appear dull, lifeless, soft, and watery. Guard against shriveled or moldy berries or baskets that are stained with juice. This means they have been held too long after picking.

Prepare: To prepare berries from this group requires pre-treatment. Ripe berries have a natural protective wax covering. It is necessary to craze this wax to allow the moisture to evaporate. Rinse the berries in cool water, pick out any stray stems or leaves, plunge them into boiling water for 30 to 60-seconds depending on the size of the fruit and the toughness of the skin. Stop the cooking action by placing them in ice water, drain them on absorbent paper toweling and place them on net in the dehydrator.

Blueberry Muffins

2 cups flour	1 egg, beaten
1 tsp salt	1/4 cup melted shortening
3 tsp baking powder	1/2 cup blueberries
1 cup milk	reconstituted in
4 Tbsp honey	1/2 cup water

Mix just enough to moisten the dry ingredients. Fill greased muffin cups 1/2 full. Bake at 400° F. for 25 to 30 minutes.

Kelly's Berry Pie

1-9" crumb or pastry crust	1 can of sweetened condensed milk
1-8 oz. package of cream cheese	1/3 cup of fresh or bottled lemon juice

Place cream cheese, sweetened condensed milk and lemon juice in blender. Mix well. Pour into the pastry shell or the graham cracker crust and refrigerate for 2 hours.

Top with:

1 cup of berries (blackberry, boysenberry, blueberry, or cherry, etc.)	1-1/2 cups of water to reconstitute berries 1 Tbsp of cornstarch

Place berries in water and simmer until reconstituted and tender. Bring to a boil, add cornstarch, stirring constantly until thickened, remove from heat, sprinkle with 1 tablespoon of sugar, refrigerate until cold, spread on top of pie and serve.

If opportunity exists to pick wildberries, take advantage of it. Take a plastic pail and a belt. Upon arrival at the berry bushes, slip the belt through the bucket bale and around your waist. It's time to go to work. Only pick 1 or 2 cups of berries before emptying the bucket. Carefully pour the berries into plastic berry cups or into a shallow cardboard box, if cups and a crate are unavailable (the weight crushes bottom berries). Vine-ripened fruit is delicious. Be sure to only pick ripe berries. Wash carefully (sorting out bad berries and stems), drain on absorbent paper towel, place on nylon net on tray, and dehydrate. If the berries are wax coated, they will have to be dipped into boiling water to check the skins. Dip them into cold water to stop the cooking action. Remove excess water by placing them on absorbent towel to blot before putting them on the trays to dry.

CARROTS

The most popular varieties are Nantes, Imperator and Danvers Half-Long. Imperator and Nantes varieties average 7-inches long and 1-1/2-inches around, tapering toward the root.

Cliptop carrots are usually the best value. If bought loose, it is easier to tell what one is getting with regard to age. Choose well-shaped, fresh-looking, small carrots without wilted foliage or cracks. The stem end is the most important place to look. If it is large and has a thick neck, the center core will be large too and it will be fibrous because that is what carries nutrients from the ground to the leaves. Look for small cores if a sweet carrot is desired, because the sugar is stored in the deep orange outside. If the stem end is black or discolored, the carrot is old.

Prepare: Wash, pare, and slice in 1/4-inch circles. Steam blanch until tender, place in ice water to cool rapidly, drain on terry towel, and place on nylon net on tray to dry. It is not necessary to steam blanch grated carrots. Just grate them and place them on the nylon net on the tray in the dryer. Do not plan long-time storage for unsteamed carrots because they will lose their carotene.

Carrot Salad

1 package of orange jello   1/2 cup grated carrots

Dissolve jello as directed on package and add 1/2 cup additional water. Set and serve.

Try some carrots sliced a little less than 1/4-inch for chips to serve with dips. Do not steam blanch them or they will not dry crisp.

As a convenience food, carrots are great. Use the grated carrots in carrot cake or cookies and use the steamed circles in stews and meat pies.

14 Karat Cake

3 cups flour   2 cups sugar
2 tsp soda   2 tsp salt
4 large eggs   1 cup nuts
1-1/2 cups grated dehydrated   1-1/2 cups oil
    carrots   2 tsp cinnamon
2-1/4 cups boiling water   1 cup raisins

Pour 2-1/4 cups boiling water over 1-1/2 cups of dehydrated carrots. Set aside for 5 minutes.

Mix dry ingredients, add oil and stir well. Add beaten eggs, mix thoroughly. Add carrots, nuts, and raisins. Mix well after each addition. Bake in a well-greased pan for 30 minutes at 350° F. and lower the temperature to 300° F. for the next 30 minutes. Remove from oven when cake tests done.

Icing

1 box powdered sugar   1-8 oz. package cream cheese
1 cube margarine   2 tsp vanilla

Cream margarine and cheese together (they should be at room temperature). Add powdered sugar and vanilla. Mix well. Spread generously on cake.

CELERY

Celery is classified by color. There are two main green varieties: Utah, developed near the Great Salt Lake (it is stringless and has a nutty flavor), and Summer Pascal which is darker green.

The prime time for celery is May with September the off-season. Remember to buy "in season" for best available prices. When buying celery, look the bunch over, top and bottom, before buying. Avoid pithy or woody looking stalks, and limp, wilted, or yellow leaves. Celery is a good source of sodium and potassium. Green varieties have more Vitamin A than blanched ones. When celery is old, the bottom butt end will turn brown and may even go black; therefore, the retailers may cut off the dark bottom surface and remove the outer stalks so the discoloration isn't noticeable. Check the bunches carefully.

Prepare: Wash, slice in 1/4-inch pieces, steam blanch, cool, dry on absorbent towel and place on net on the tray to dehydrate. To prepare the leaves for stews it is only necessary to wash thoroughly and place on the tray to dry.

Celery may be powdered for seasoning or added to stews and casseroles.

CEREAL AND CRACKER CRISPING

When humidity is high and granola, prepared cereals, chips, or crackers become soft, place them in the dehydrator for 30 minutes to recrisp them.

CHERRIES

Bing is the most popular sweet cherry. Lambert and Tartarian are also good varieties. The Royal Ann is a good drying variety. Montmorency is the leading sour cherry used for pies and freezing.

Sour cherries are in season from mid-June to mid-August. June is peak season for other varieties. Sour cherries are hard to find in some areas.

The Royal Ann is heart-shaped, with yellowish flesh and a red blush. It bruises easily and doesn't look as appetizing as the Bing cherry when dried; however, it does have good flavor. Royal Ann's are a little tart as snack foods, but make good dessert recipes.

When buying Bing cherries, be sure to select dark-red, firm cherries. If they are light-red and small, they are unripe and will be hard and sour. Look for plump, shiny, maroon-colored fruit with green stems. Avoid dark-colored stems, sticky fruits, and dull, soft appearance—mold may be forming. For a longer storage life, cherries should be refrigerated. Bing cherries make good snack foods. They can be substituted for or used with raisins in cake and cookie recipes.

If twins or doubles meet the quality standards, and are less expensive, they are a good buy. The disadvantage is the extra time consumed in pitting them.

Prepare: Wash carefully, remove stems, cut in half and remove pits. Place on nylon net on dehydrator tray and dry. Place the skin side down on the net so the juice will remain in the hollow and nutrients will not be lost. When using a commercial cherry pitter, place the cherry with the skin side down rather than the hole so juices will not be lost.

Cherries may be dipped in boiling water for 30 seconds to craze the skin, placed in ice water to stop the cooking action and dried with the pit. They look like miniature prunes when they are dry. This is a time saver when preparing them for snack foods.

Cherry Pie

Make pastry for a two-crust, 9-inch pie.

Mix together:

1-1/3 cups sugar	1-1/2 tsp almond extract
5 Tbsp flour	1/2 tsp cinnamon

Mix lightly with 3 cups of cherries that have been rehydrated in 1-1/2 cups of water. Pour into a pastry-lined pie pan, dot with 1 tablespoon butter, cover with top crust and bake at 400° F. for 35 minutes or until crust is nicely browned and juice is bubbling through the slits. This is best when served while slightly warm.

CHICKEN

Left-over chicken may be dehydrated to use for camping, hiking, snacking, etc.

Prepare: When the chicken is cold, trim all fat off from it, place it on the dehydrator tray, and dry. It is best to store chicken in the refrigerator until ready for use to prevent rancidity. To save it for a camping trip, it would be wise to freeze it and take it out just prior to leaving for the trip.

It is good to just munch on as a snack. It can be reconstituted to make chicken a la king, meat pie, etc.

CITRUS PEELS

Check each orange, lemon, or grapefruit before dehydrating the peel. If color has been added, they should be stamped "Color added." The dye has a tendency to make the rind bitter.

Prepare: Wash and dry. Grate on a grater until the white membrane is reached, but do not grate into it. Place grated peel on net, and place on tray in dehydrator. If storage time is to be short, grate the peel. For long time storage, the peel will have a stronger flavor if it is peeled in strips of 1/4-inch. Do not cut into the white membrane. Store in strips and put into the blender to chop just prior to using.

For a special treat, place pieces of orange peel in equal amounts of water and honey and let stand overnight. Use 1 tablespoon of water to 1 tablespoon of honey and add 1 tablespoon of rind. Store in the refrigerator in a closed container.

At the YWCA Drying Club potluck dinner, the dried apple pie with dehydrated orange peel was the hit of the dinner.

COCONUT

There are many varieties of wild and cultivated coconuts. To pick a good fresh one, shake it, and choose one that contains liquid. Keep it refrigerated until it is dehydrated.

Prepare: The first step is to drain the milk. Look for the three "eyes" at the pointed end, and puncture one or two of these spots with an ice pick or small screwdriver. If the milk is to be saved to drink, hold the coconut over a bowl to catch it. Next, crack the shell open with a hammer. Work on a wooden board or outside on the cement. After the shell is removed, pare the wrinkly brown skin away with a vegetable parer. Grate the coconut onto plastic wrap on the dehydrator tray, and place in dryer. Watch carefully—do not overdry the coconut.

Moisture does not need to be added to coconut. Use it in granola, fruit salads, sprinkled on top of banana cream cake or pie, cookies, etc.

COMFREY

Comfrey is the only land plant discovered that contains Vitamin B_{12}. The root is white, fleshy, and juicy. The leaves are large, oval and hairy. Harvest comfrey just before it blooms. Leave about 2 inches on the stem stub or the newly-forming crown will be damaged. Cut the leaves at the end of the day when their food value is high.

Prepare: Comfrey leaves are tender so handle them carefully so as not to bruise them. Separate the leaves from the stems. Wash, drain, and place on separate trays. Because of the difference in drying times for the leaves and the stems it is essential to keep them separated. It is also more convenient to store them separately. Slice stems 1/4-inch thick; and if leaves are really large, fold them in half and cut out the heavy center stem. Comfrey dries hard, so it is necessary to have it cut small for grinding.

Comfrey is a good source of lysine when ground and added to bread or muffins. It can be roasted, ground, and used as a coffee substitute.

CORN

Burpee's Honeycross, Ilini Xtra-Sweet, Golden Cross Bantam, Burpee's Golden Bantam are good in yellow varieties, and Stowell's Evergreen Hybrid, Burpee's White Evergreen, and Country Gentlemen are white varieties that can be grown in home gardens.

May through September are peak months for corn. As soon as corn is picked, the sugar starts converting to starch. The fresher corn is more sweet. Ears of corn should not be piled high because this generates heat. If it is necessary to keep corn for a short time, put the husked ears in transparent bags and keep at 40° to 50° F. Ears with dented kernels show a loss of moisture, and will probably taste tough. When buying corn, look for fresh green husks and check the stem end for dryness or discolor. The kernels should be well-filled, milky, and tender.

Prepare: Husk corn, remove silk, wash in cold water, trim any bad spots, and place in a steamer. Steam corn on the cob until the milk has set (3-10 minutes according to individual desire), and place in ice water to stop cooking process. Cut kernels from the cob, making sure that the cut is not too deep to get any cob. Place on the net on the dryer tray, and dehydrate.

Corn may be used as a vegetable, or it may be ground and used as cornmeal. When trying home ground dried corn, cut down the measurements in the recipe. Since it does not contain fiber, this cornmeal requires more moisture than purchased cornmeal.

Corn Pancakes

To be served with syrup and ham for breakfast.

2/3 cup dried corn	2 tsp baking powder
1-1/2 cups boiling water	1 tsp baking soda
(let stand 5 minutes)	2 tsp sugar
1 cup buttermilk	1 egg
1 cup yellow corn meal (0/4 cup	1 Tbsp vegetable oil
dehydrated ground corn)	1 tsp salt

Drain the corn and reserve the water. Place in a medium-sized mixing bowl; add remaining ingredients, except milk, and mix well. Lightly oil a heavy skillet or griddle, and heat to medium temperature (until a drop of water sizzles on the surface). Add milk mixture to corn mixture, and stir it in quickly; mixture will be thin and foamy. The reserved water may be needed at this time. Drop the corn batter by tablespoonsful onto the griddle, cook until browned on bottom, and bubbles are breaking on the surface. Turn and brown on the other side. Remove and serve. Before placing batter on griddle, restir the batter to thoroughly blend the ingredients. This makes about 20 3-1/2-inch cakes.

One cup of whole milk, plus 1 tablespoon of lemon juice, may be substituted for the buttermilk. Put the lemon juice in the milk, and let it stand for 5 minutes. Yogurt and water may also be substituted for buttermilk.

Corn Crisps

Blend in blender until smooth:

3 cups fresh tomatoes, quartered	2 Tbsp safflower oil
	1 tsp salt
1/4 cup onion, quartered	1 tsp chili powder

Slowly add 2 cups of ground dried corn to the ingredients in the blender. When the mixture is the consistency of thick malt, pour it onto plastic wrap like fruit leather, spread to within 1/2-inch of the edge, and place in dehydrator until crisp. Pour it to a depth of 1/4-inch. This may be used for chips for dips.

Parched Corn

1/3 square of margarine. *Do*   2 cups dried corn
    not use butter—it will burn.

Heat margarine until melted, add corn, reduce heat to low and cook, stirring constantly. When the corn has turned brown, and has puffed up, it is done. It takes about 10 minutes. Be careful not to scorch it.

Kenny's Corn Pudding

1 cup dried corn reconstituted in 2 cups boiling water	1 tsp sugar
	1-1/2 tsp salt
	1/8 tsp pepper
2 eggs	1 Tbsp melted butter
1 cup evaporated milk	

Place all ingredients in a blender. Blend until the ingredients are well blended, but not completely pureed. Pour the corn mixture into a well-greased 1-quart baking dish; place in a shallow pan of water, and bake at 350° F. for 50 minutes. For a brown crust, remove the dish from the water for the last 15 minutes of baking time. The pudding is done when the center is firm.

COATING MIX

To be used for coating chicken, fish, etc. by shaking in a plastic bag. The kind can be changed according to individual taste.

To make the bread crumbs, purchase a loaf of day-old bread from the bread store and dehydrate it. It takes about 45 minutes for it to be toasted just right. Place several slices into a plastic bag and roll with a rolling pin until fine crumbs are obtained. These crumbs may be kept in the deepfreeze, and used for poultry dressing, casserole toppings, meatloaf extender, etc.

Italian Flavored Coating Mix

4 cups dehydrated bread
   crumbs
1/2 tsp garlic powder
1/2 cup Safflower oil
1/2 tsp fresh ground
   pepper

1/2 cup grated cheese
   (Longhorn or cheddar)
1 tsp salt
1 tsp oregano

Combine and mix all of the ingredients thoroughly; refrigerate or freeze. The mixture remains soft when stored in the freezer and will keep indefinitely. Remove desired amount, place in plastic bag, and shake until meat is well coated. This makes about 5 cups.

CROUTONS

Use day old bread, slice into desired size, place on net and dry. One hour is sufficient if doing just small amounts (1 loaf of bread). Season croutons just before using. They may be stored in the deepfreeze to extend their storage life.

Varieties may be obtained by purchasing different types of bread, such as sourdough, pumpernickle, or the bread may be seasoned with any desired flavor.

Melt 2 tablespoons of butter in a skillet. Add a choice of seasonings—1/4 teaspoon garlic or onion powder, 1/4 teaspoon dill weed, or 1/2 teaspoon poultry seasoning. Add 4 cups of dehydrated croutons and toss lightly until evenly coated. A dash of Parmesan, just before removing from pan, adds a special treat for cheese lovers.

CUCUMBERS

Burpee's Sunnybrook has only a few seeds. Burpee Hybrid, Improved Long Green, Marketer, and Armenian cucumbers are some good varieties.

Prepare: Wash, slice slightly under 1/4-inch, place on trays and dry. Cucumbers are good used as chips for dips.

When water is added to cucumbers, they become tough, therefore, do not plan to use them in salads or spiced with vinegar and seasoning.

Use small cucumbers so the seeds will not be too large. Personal preference determines whether or not they are peeled.

Puree cucumbers, pour on plastic wrap and dry as leather. Dry quite crisp, remove from plastic wrap, place in blender and powder to be used as seasoning on green salads when cucumbers are not "in season."

To steam or not to steam is up to the individual.

DATE SUGAR

Date sugar is sugar in its most natural form. There are over 100 varieties of dates grown in Coachella Valley, California.

Fresh dates are available from September through May with the peak month being November. Look for plump, golden brown, smooth skinned dates with a glossy appearance. Avoid dull or shriveled dates. Dates may be added to leathers to provide sweetening. Date sugar can be used to sweeten yogurt, desserts prepared with whipping cream, etc.

Prepare: Remove pits, cut into small pieces, place on trays, and dry. After they are thoroughly dry, put them into the blender and make the sugar.

DILL

The basic difference between dill seed and dillweed is in the bitterness; the seed has a slightly bitter taste while the weed has a delicate aroma and flavor.

The dill plant is umbrella shaped and is light green with one main stem. It has a yellow flower. Leaves are harvested about 8 weeks after seeding. Dill weed reaches its flavoring peak at the bloom stage. For best flavor, this is the time to harvest it. To harvest seeds, wait until they're light brown, then cut the umbels and dry them. Cut during the early morning hours to prevent loss of seeds, place in dehydrator with only the fan running. Use plastic wrap to catch the seeds as they fall. It may be necessary to use the heating element to preserve the color and flavor of the dill leaves if the weather is cool.

EGGS

A spray-dry process is required to produce quality dehydrated eggs.

EGGPLANT

Black Beauty, Black Magic, and Burpee Hybrid Eggplant are some varieties to look for.

The fruits are best when the skin has a high gloss. If picked young, the seeds will be small and hardly noticeable. This is desirable for dehydrating. The cap should look fresh and green. Avoid flabby, shriveled, or dark brown spots on the surface indicating signs of decay. Peak harvest time is in July and August.

Prepare: Wash, peel, dice, and steam until tender. Place in cold water, drain, and place in dehydrator.

Eggplant Casserole

2 cups eggplant reconstituted in 3 cups water	3 eggs, beaten
2 tsp Lawry's seasoned salt	A dash of tabasco sauce or
1/2 cup chopped green onion	1 Tbsp chopped green chilies
1 Tbsp margarine	4 Tbsp parmesan cheese
1/2 cup shredded cheddar cheese	paprika

Saute onion in margarine, drain eggplant, combine all ingredients except parmesan cheese and paprika, and place in oiled baking dish. Top with parmesan cheese and paprika. Bake at 350° F. for 30 to 40 minutes. Serve.

FIGS

Calimyrna, Mission and Kodata figs are good varieties for dehydrating—Calimyrna is much sweeter.

Mission is a dark purple fig, and must be almost black to be really ripe. Kodota has a thick green skin that turns yellow when ripe, and it doesn't have too many seeds. Calimyrna has a smooth thick yellowish-green skin and is large. Fresh figs are very perishable. Size doesn't indicate ripeness or maturity. In order to be good and sweet, figs must be really ripe. If they can be left on the tree to partly dry this is preferable. Large figs must be cut to allow drying without fermentation. The fig is fertilized by wasps. The wasps carry yeast with them and this is what causes fermentation of overripe figs. Avoid bruised fruit. Fresh figs are available from June through October.

To catch falling figs and protect them from insect infestation, it is possible to place a sheet under the tree by suspending it from the lower branches. To protect the figs from birds, it may be necessary to put net over the top.

Prepare: Wash, trim, cut off stem, quarter or cut into eights depending on size, place with skin side down on net on tray, and place in dehydrator.

To serve stewed figs for breakfast, add 1-1/2 cups of boiling water to each cup of figs, and simmer until they are tender. Add a little sugar or honey if desired. Serve.

Fig Bars

> 1 cup dried figs   1 Tbsp dried lemon peel
> Reconstitute above in 1-3/4 cups hot water

Blend in blender with:

> 1-1/2 cups sugar or 1 cup honey

Combine following ingredients:

> 2-1/2 cups flour   1/2 cup sugar
> 1/2 tsp salt   1 tsp baking powder
> 1 cube of margarine

Mix together until crumbly. Pat approximately 2 cups of this mixture into the bottom of a 9 x 13-inch oblong pan (reserve the remaining mix for the top crust). Pour fig mixture over dough—spread evenly. Sprinkle on the reserved crumbs. Bake at 350° F. for 15 minutes, or until lightly browned.

FISH

Fresh fish have clear, bulging eyes; elastic, firm flesh; reddish pink gills, and they are free from strong odor. Salmon is the easiest to dry. Rainbow trout (depending on size) may be dried whole or in halves.

The temperature range should be 140° F. to 150° F. for fish.

Prepare: Remove the head, fins, tail, viscera, and kidney (the dark red mass along the backbone). Wash the body cavity with cold running water to remove as much blood as possible. Cut fish into desired size pieces. Do not make the pieces more than 1/2-inch thick for more even drying.

There are two basic methods for salting fish and drying it: The dry cure and the brine solution.

To dry cure—Mix the following ingredients:

2 cups salt	1 tsp fresh ground pepper
1 Tbsp saltpeter	1 tsp garlic powder
1/2 tsp onion powder	1 cup brown sugar

Dry curing is especially good for large fish. Spices may be added if desired; such as dill, cloves, bay leaves, etc. Mix all ingredients well, and let them blend for 12 to 18 hours before placing on fish. One pound of dry cure will give a medium strong cure for 10 pounds of fish.

After washing fish, pat dry and sprinkle with dry cure. Layer the fish in a glass container. Place 1/4-inch of dry cure in the bottom of the container. Place a layer of fish over the salt. Cover the fish with a 1/4-inch layer of salt. Alternate layers of fish and salt. Cover the container with a cloth and place in the refrigerator. Leave small fish in salt from 1 to 12 hours; larger fish up to 24 hours, depending upon weather, size of fish, fatness, and length of time fish are to be preserved before use. A brine will form in the bottom of the container. Remove fish from the refrigerator, brush off excess salt, place on nylon netting on dehydrator trays, and dry. Fish should be firm to hard with no soft spots. Store in an airtight container in the refrigerator for short time storage and the deepfreeze for longer storage.

A basic fish brine requires approximately 1/2 cup of salt per 1 quart of water. If seasoning is desired, it may be added to the basic brine. If garlic flavor is desired, it may be added and is more convenient in the liquid form. For people on a restricted salt diet, potassium chloride may be substituted. It is available from a chemical supply house. Be sure to specify food grade quality. Potassium chloride may be substituted for sodium chloride (table salt) with the dehydrating process because dehydration is the preserving technique. Potassium chloride can not be substituted when salting is the method of preservation.

Seasoned Brine

1 pint of cold water	1/2 tsp onion powder or
3 Tbsp salt	liquid, if available, for
1/4 cup of molasses	easier mixing
1/2 tsp Krazy Mixed-Up Salt *	1/4 tsp fresh ground pepper
(a mixture of herbs, spices & salt)	

Dissolve the salt in the water first, then add the other ingredients and mix thoroughly. Soak the fish for 1 hour, rinse off when it gets a velvety sheen and dehydrate.

This is enough brine to salt 3 pounds of fish.

1 pint of cold water	1/4 cup of brown sugar
3 Tbsp salt	1/4 tsp tabasco
1 Tbsp soy sauce	1/4 tsp fresh ground pepper

Follow directions above. This is enough brine to salt 3 pounds of fish.

Rainbow Trout—Fillet the trout and use either of the above mixtures or develop a new one. It is fun to experiment. Liquid smoke may be added if desired.

To fillet trout, remove the skin by pulling from the head to the tail. It is best to remove fins by pulling them out rather than cutting them, as the bones will be removed with the fin. There is a lateral line about one-third of the distance down the side of the fish which runs the entire length of the fish. With a knife, gently separate the fish at this line. First remove the upper one-third of the meat from the bones, and then pull the lower two-thirds away

*Distributed by Haddon House Food Products, Inc., Jane's Krazy Mixed-Up Salt.

from the ribs. Some ribs may break and cling to the fillet, but they may be pulled out easily. Repeat this procedure on the other side of the fish.

Salmon—Cut the fish in chunks. It is not necessary to remove the skin or bones. The small bones become edible and the larger bones can be removed at the time of eating. Soak the fish in one of the brine solutions for one hour (the scales will come off in the brine solution), rinse off the fish when it gets a velvety sheen and dehydrate. The fish will have a brown satiny texture when it is done. It will be firm and hard with no soft spots.

Tui Chubs—The fish should be frozen overnight then placed in a salt brine for 24 hours in the refrigerator and dried. They have many small bones but with this process the bones become edible.

FRUIT LEATHER

Any fruits that are overripe for dehydrating may be used to make fruit leathers. Fruit leather is good for campers, hikers, travel, sack-lunch, after-school snacks, quick pick-up, and TV snacks.

Fruit that is too soft for dehydrating in slices, or fruit that can have blemishes trimmed off may be used for fruit leather. This does not mean fruit that is souring.

Bottled fruit or canned fruit may be drained and used for leather. Save the juice for punch, puree the fruit, and make leather. Fruit may be pureed and kept in the freezer for making leather at a more convenient time. Just let the fruit thaw, place on plastic wrap, and dry. Thick puree requires more drying time than thin puree. One-quarter inch is a good thickness for efficient drying. Fruit leather needs to be labeled before storing because after storage it all looks alike. The only way to identify it is by the taste test. Fruit leather is concentrated, and so the calories are high for a small piece.

Prepare: Wash fruit, remove pits and peels that would be objectionable (fuzzy peaches), cut in slices, place in blender, and puree. Most fruits will not need sweetner added. Sugar tends to make leather grainy in long time storage, so it is better to use honey or corn syrup if additional sweetner is desired. Pour and spread to within 1/2-inch of the edge of plastic wrap. Make the edge a little more than 1/4-inch, and make the middle only 1/4-inch. It will dry at the edge more rapidly than in the middle; therefore, by making the edge thicker it permits more uniform drying. Place the tray in the dehydrator to dry. Test the center of the leather by touching it with a finger. If it is sticky, let it dry longer. It usually takes about 12 hours for fruit leather to dry. Humidity, moisture content of fruit, and thickness of leather affect drying time. Remove the fruit leather from the plastic wrap while it is still warm. Place it on a new piece of plastic wrap and roll for storage. It has a tendency to remain sticky if the plastic on which it was dried is reused. Label the roll and place it in a large paper bag, a pillow case, a large plastic bag, or in the deepfreeze for long time storage. Roll the leather like jelly rolls, letting the plastic keep it from touching itself to prevent sticking.

Fruit leather will be used mostly for snack foods. Fruit leather that is too brittle may be softened by adding a few drops of water to a plastic bag and placing the leather inside. Close the bag tightly, and let it stand for 8 hours to allow the over-dry leather to absorb the added moisture. Leather may be reconstituted for use in malts, shakes, ice cream, or as flavoring for yogurt. It makes a tasty dessert when added to vanilla pie and pudding mix. Use 1 cup of broken pieces of leather, and 3/4 cup of water. Let it stand for 10 minutes, and then blend it to malt consistency in the blender. Remember this is concentrated fruit. For a malt, one cup of fruit would make 2 quarts.

To make *apple leather*, the apples should be washed thoroughly, quartered, cored, but not peeled, and placed in a blender. Apples are the only fruit that require moisture to be added when blending. They are hard, and it is best to put one tablespoon of water or a fruit juice with just a few slices of apple to get the blender started. Then add the remainder of the fruit. Two cups of puree will fill one 12 x 12-inch square tray with leather.

The natural pectin from the apple gels the juice and makes a thick leather. Try two apples per cup of juice, or two apples with one cup of orange segments. Peel the orange, remove excess membrane and seeds, and blend.

Some good combinations:

Apples with cinnamon, nutmeg, or cloves.
Apples with tangerine juice.
Apples with mandarin orange segments.
Apples with orange juice.

Clingstone cherry plums make great jelly, and the pulp may then be put through a colander to remove skins and pits for excellent *plum leather.* Cook the plums for 5 minutes to soften the fruit on the stone. Place in colander over a pan to catch the juice. Make jelly from the juice and make leather from the pulp.

Strawberry/rhubarb leather is a favorite with many people. Rhubarb must be cooked before it is pureed, or it will be stringy. Place rhubarb and about 1 tablespoon of water (just enough to get it started to cook) into pan and let simmer 2 or 3 minutes. Place 2 cups washed berries, 1 cup stewed rhubarb, and 2 tablespoons honey into blender, and puree. Pour onto plastic wrap on tray to dry.

Pumpkin leather is made by steaming the pumpkin. Measure 2 cups of pumpkin, 2 tablespoons of honey, 1/2 teaspoon pumpkin pie spice and put into blender. Puree, and pour onto plastic wrap to dry.

Mincemeat leather is made by spreading mincemeat pie filling onto plastic wrap. (1/4-inch thick). Place in dehydrator and dry. This will take longer to dry than just plain fruit leathers.

Cranberry leather has many variations. Puree in blender, 1 cup cranberries, 1/2 cup unpeeled (cored) apples, 1 cup pitted dates, and 1 cup miniature marshmallows. Spread on plastic wrap and dry.
Variations: Use 1 cup pureed cranberries and 1/2 cup unpeeled apples, plus 2 tablespoons honey. Use 1 peeled orange with seeds removed, 1 cup cranberries, and 2 tablespoons honey.

Pineapple leather is very good. Puree 2 cups of fresh pineapple (cut into cubes) in blender. Pour onto plastic wrap and dry. Canned pineapple makes good leather also.

After making grape juice, save the pulp and press it through a colander to make *grape/apple leather.* A tasty leather can be made by combining 1-1/2 cups of grape pulp and 1 unpeeled, cored apple. Puree in blender, and dry on plastic wrap.

Try adding nuts to *apricot leather*, but do not plan for long time storage because nuts will go rancid.

Banana leather with 1/4 cup of lemon juice, 1 tablespoon of honey, and a little grated lemon rind makes an interesting combination.

To retain a brighter color in fruits with a high vitamin C content, it is advisable to boil the puree for 2 minutes, let it cool, and pour onto plastic wrap to dry.

The above examples are a few favorite combinations for fruit leather, but there are many more. Imagination, experimentation, and taste test create many new combinations.

There are many ways of storing leather. Each individual has to find the right way for the individual's climate, storage conditions, etc. Some instructions say, "Never store leather in the refrigerator." After two years of storage in the meat dehydrator of the refrigerator, the leather is still in excellent condition. While learning about storage conditions, it is advisable to check to make sure the leather is not being attacked by bugs or going moldy. It is too good to waste.

GRANOLA

Granola is the health food store novelty that today is a common ingredient in most every kitchen. It is not just a breakfast food, but is used in cookies, snacks, desserts, stuffings, muffins, breads, pies, vegetable dishes, and meat dishes.

Once grains are milled, they oxidize quickly. It is possible to store them in the freezer if properly packaged. Mark each bag with its contents and date. Toasted wheat germ may be added at the time of serving. Store unhulled sesame seeds in a tightly-closed container and keep cool and dry. Hulled seeds need to be refrigerated and used promptly. Sunflower seeds last longer when unshelled. Because of the time factor, it isn't always feasible to use unshelled sunflower seeds. Store shelled seeds in the refrigerator in closed containers. Nuts, of course, go rancid and must be kept under refrigeration. They too keep better if kept in the shell. Watch the ingredients carefully, and keep a good balance of nutrition and calories. Unfortunately it is easy to choose foods with high calories and low nutrients, and this must be avoided.

Prepare: The first step in making granola is to decide what ingredients should go into it. To make granola saves money, allows a choice of ingredients, makes it more fresh, and allows individual creativity. Assemble all ingredients. Make a basic granola, and it can then be used as many different varieties.

Basic Granola Recipe

1/2 cup untoasted wheat germ	3/4 tsp salt
4 cups quick or	1/2 cup honey
old-fashioned oatmeal	1/3 cup vegetable oil
1/2 cup sesame seed	1/2 tsp vanilla

The basic recipe may be made from 1 cup each of oats, wheat flakes, rye flakes, and triticale flakes. The other ingredients remain the same. Granola may be changed with regard to other ingredients also, but remember that if too many things are added, it will necessitate additional oil and honey.

Measure oil first, then honey, and it will not stick to the cup. Add the vanilla and mix thoroughly. Pour over dry ingredients. Let stand 1/2 to 1 hour so oats will absorb the flavor. Place on plastic wrap on trays and dry for from 1 to 3 hours according to personal taste. This makes 3, one square foot trays when spread evenly over tray to a depth of 1/2-inch. Adding the dry ingredients to the wet ingredients makes a crunchier granola. Using date sugar and sea salt, and adding them to the liquid ingredients, will make a coated frosty granola.

For variations:

Diced dried bananas and walnuts may be added before serving.

Chopped dried apples and cinnamon may be added.

Slivered almonds and fresh dried coconut may be added.

Berries—strawberry/raspberry/blackberry, etc. may be added with milk.

Everyone in the family can choose a favorite granola breakfast. Let individual taste be the guide.

D.D.'s Afterschool Snack

Blend until smooth:

3/4 cup oil	1/2 tsp salt
2/3 cup honey	2 tsp vanilla
3 large apples, cored, peeled and diced	

1/4 small lemon peeled   1/4 tsp grated lemon rind
   (be sure to take out seeds)

Mix in:

3 cups rolled oats   1 cup raisins

Let stand for 1 hour to allow the oats to soak up flavors. Drop by the teaspoonful onto plastic wrap, place on dryer shelves, and dry. Remove the cookies while they are soft and eat. To prevent rancidity keep them refrigerated.

Granola Meatloaf

1 cup basic granola   1/4 tsp tabasco sauce
1 pound ground beef   1 tsp salt
2 onions diced (small)   1/4 tsp pepper
1 cup canned spinach

Combine all ingredients and form into a loaf. Bake at 350° F. for 50 minutes.

Granola Fruit and Cream

1 cup of granola   12 banana slices chopped
   (a nut variety)   2 cups heavy cream whipped
1/4 cup lemon juice   3 Tbsp date sugar
12 apple slices chopped   1/4 cup honey
12 pear slices chopped   1/8 tsp nutmeg
12 dates pitted and chopped

Soak the granola in the lemon juice for 1/2 hour and then add fruits. Add nutmeg to honey and heat until it is fluid. Pour it over the granola mixture. Place it in the refrigerator to cool for 1 hour. When ready to serve, whip the cream until it is stiff, add the date sugar, fold in the granola mixture, and spoon into sherbet dishes.

It is possible to substitute different fruits according to individual taste in this recipe.

Granola Crust Dessert

Line a 9 x 13-inch oblong pan with 2 cups of granola made with nuts, and mixed with 1 tablespoon of melted butter. Reserve about 1/4 cup of the granola. Whip 1 pint of whipping cream, add 1, 10-1/2 ounce package of miniature marshmallows, and pour it into the granola crust. Spread 1 can of cherry pie filling over the top of the cream mixture, and sprinkle with the reserved granola. Chill 1 hour and serve.

Peanut Butter Candy

1 cup peanut butter	1-1/4 cups instant nonfat
1 cup corn syrup	dry milk
1-1/4 cups powdered sugar	

Mix all ingredients well. Form into balls and roll in granola (a nut variety made from fine oats). Chill before serving. If the granola is coarse, it should be ground to the consistency of graham cracker crumbs.

GRAPES

Thompson Seedless, Monukka, King's Ruby are good varieties to dehydrate. Any seedless variety should be good.

Choose fully ripe grapes to take advantage of the sweetness. The grapes should be firmly attached to the stems. Dry, brown stems indicate storage for too long a time. Grapes have a natural wax coating. If they are shiny, they have had too much handling. The season runs from June into November with peak season in September and October. Store grapes in the refrigerator until they are ready to process.

Prepare: Wash, remove stems, plunge into boiling water for 30 seconds, place into ice water to stop cooking process, dry on terry towel, place on net on trays, and dehydrate. Twelve to 14 hours in the dehydrator, and like magic, golden raisins appear.

After removing the seeds from seeded varieties of grapes, all that remains after dehydration is the skin. It has a good flavor, but it is not worth the effort to prepare.

ICE CREAM

Use any dehydrated fruits or berries to make ice cream. Just add them to the milk as it goes into the refrigerator to stand undisturbed for 10 minutes. Use cubes or small slices cut in thirds for an even distribution throughout the ice cream.

Four-Quart Freezer

6 rennet tablets	1/4 cup cold water
2-2/3 cups sugar	2 quarts milk (not canned)
2-2/3 cups heavy cream (whipping)	1-1/2 Tbsp vanilla

Dissolve rennet tablets in cold water. Combine remaining ingredients and heat to lukewarm (110° F.). Add 1-1/2 cups of broken fruit or berry pieces, rehydrated in 1/2 cup of water (strawberry, apricot, raspberry, blackberry, blueberry, peach, pumpkin leather, etc.). Stir in the dissolved rennet tablets quickly, pour into freezer, place in refrigerator, and let stand undisturbed for 10 minutes. Put into hand or electric freezer and freeze.

JERKY

Brisket, flank steak, or round steak can be used to make jerky. Brisket costs more per pound but has very little waste. Jerky can also be made from bear, deer, elk, and buffalo. When preparing jerky from game meat, it is important to see that the meat is clean and kept cold. As a precaution against diseased meat, it should be stored in the deepfreeze at 0° F. for 30 days before eating.

Prepare: Remove all visible fat, and slice into thin strips 1/4-inch by 1/2-inch. Cut the meat with the grain to avoid shattering. The meat is easier to cut when it has been partially frozen. Marinate in desired sauce. Place in a colander to drip dry for 10 minutes, and lay on dehydrator trays to dry. Do not overlap, but leave plenty of space for circulation of air. When jerky is chewy but not tough or brittle it is ready to be stored in a glass jar. It takes approximately 3 to 4 hours if the temperature is maintained at 140° F. to 150° F. For long time storage, jerky retains more flavor if stored at refrigerator temperature.

Note: A salt substitute may be used if a person's diet is restricted from salt.

Condensation will cause mold to grow on jerky. To prevent this, holes can be punched in the top of the lid on the jar; however, it is then susceptible to contamination. It is better to store the jerky in a bottle with a sealed lid in a spot where there is even temperature.

Natural Flavor Marinade

1 pound of meat	1-1/2 tsp salt
1/4 tsp pepper	1/4 tsp garlic powder or crushed garlic

Put the salt directly onto the meat first as it removes some of the moisture. Let the meat marinate for 1 hour. If a stronger flavor is desired, let the meat marinate for a longer time. If the time is extended to 4 hours, then the meat and marinade should be kept in the refrigerator.

Smoke Flavor Marinade

1 Tbsp Liquid Smoke	1 package of Schilling
1 tsp salt	Meat Marinade
4 pounds of meat	3/4 cup of water

Mix according to the directions on the marinade package, and then add 1 teaspoon of salt and 1 tablespoon of liquid smoke. Let it stand for 10 minutes. Put the marinade in a 9 x 13-inch oblong glass dish, add 3/4 cup of water, and let it stand 1/2 hour, stirring occasionally. Put strips of meat into the sauce and marinate for 1/2 hour. Make sure all pieces of meat are covered. After 15 minutes, turn each piece of meat so that the other side has an equal opportunity to absorb the marinade. This is sufficient marinade to season a 4 pound brisket; however, it is necessary to marinate 3 different times to make sure all pieces of meat get equal coverage. Drain, place on trays, and dry.

Soy sauce can be substituted for the liquid smoke for those who are wary of the effects with regard to carcinogens.

Sweet-Sour Marinade

1/2 tsp liquid onion	1/2 tsp salt
1/4 cup brown sugar	1/3 cup vinegar
1 cup pineapple juice	1 Tbsp soy sauce
1/4 cup water	4 pounds of meat

Put all of the ingredients into a 9 x 13-inch oblong glass pan. Mix well. Let it stand for 1/2 hour, stirring occasionally. Put the strips of meat into the marinade and marinate for 1 hour. After 1/2 hour turn each piece of meat with tongs so that both sides absorb the flavoring. Drain and place on trays to dehydrate.

MELONS

Any food with a high water content is so concentrated, after it is dehydrated, that the experience of tasting it may not be pleasant. Melons acutally look beautiful, but they are much too strong to be appetizing to most people. Try some!

MEAT

Use any left-over meat available to prepare for campouts, convenience foods, and lazy days.

If there is a good supply of Sunday roast left after dinner, cube or slice the left-over meat to make stew, pie, or chow mein.

Prepare: After the meat is cool, remove all fat, place on trays, and dry. Store in an air-tight container at 40° F.

To reconstitute, use about 1 cup of meat and 2 cups of water. Simmer in unsalted water until tender, then add seasonings. This is an excellent way to store meat for camping.

MILK

To have high-quality dehydrated milk, it is necessary to use a spray-dry process.

MINT

Mint plants have square stems. The leaves grow on the stems in twos, one on each side of the stem. The flowers grow on spikes at the end of the stem above the scented leaves. Spearmint is not as strongly flavored as peppermint and is the mint most commonly used in sauces and jellies.

Prepare: Pick leaves, wash carefully, pat dry, and place in dehydrator. Do not turn on the heating element. Use only the fan.

MUSHROOMS

Look for mushrooms with the cap curling over the edge and covering the dark underneath part. If the cap doesn't curl under, it means the mushroom has lost some of its moisture and will be hard and tough to cut. The peak season for mushrooms is November through April.

Prepare: Do not wash or peel mushrooms. Brush dirt off carefully, or wipe lightly with a damp cloth to clean them. Remove a thin slice from the bottom of the stem. Cut the mushrooms vertically into thirds or fourths depending upon the size. Place on the dehydrator trays on net. Do not steam. Do not discard the stem, but slice so that the stem remains attached to the button.

To reconstitute, place the desired amount of mushrooms into a bowl. Just barely cover with warm water; let them soak for 5 minutes. If the recipe does not call for the liquid they were soaked in, pour it into a stock pot for future use.

NECTARINES

There are clingstone and freestone varieties. Sun Grand is an early freestone and LeGrand and Gold King are clingstone varieties.

The peak nectarine season is in July and early August. Look for firm, plump, well-formed fruit with a yellow skin and a bright red cheek. Nectarines must be picked mature to have good sweet flavor. Dull colored or hard green fruit will shrivel instead of ripening. Avoid nectarines that have been rained on at harvest time because they spoil rapidly.

Prepare: Wash carefully, peel (if desired), remove the stones, slice in 3/8-inch slices, dip into ascorbic acid, drain in a colander, place on net and dehydrate.

Nectarine Pudding

1-1/4 cups instant nonfat
  dry milk
2 cups cold water
1/2 tsp vanilla

1/4 cup sugar
1/4 cup cornstarch
1 tsp butter or margarine
1/2 cup nectarine slices
  rehydrated in 1/4 cup
  of water

Stir milk, sugar, and cornstarch thoroughly. Gradually add water; bring to a boil, and cook until thickened. Remove from the heat, and stir in vanilla, butter, and nectarines. Pour into serving dishes, and refrigerate until set. Garnish with whipped cream.

NOODLES

When making noodles, do an extra amount to dehydrate as a convenience food or a snack food.

2 cups unbleached white flour (May need more to make stiff dough)	2 eggs, well beaten 1/2 cup buttermilk 1 tsp salt
1/4 cup soy flour, optional (reduce white flour)	1/4 cup wheat germ, optional (reduce white flour)

Beat eggs, add other liquid, stir, and work in the flours with hands. Divide dough into 3 parts. Roll out each piece as thin as possible on a lightly-floured cloth-covered board. Sprinkle flour lightly on top of the rolled dough, and roll up dough as for jelly roll. With a thin sharp knife, cut into strips 1/4-inch to 1/2-inch in width. Shake out the strips and place on the dehydrator tray to dry (use net). This makes about 6 cups of noodles. Place in a plastic bag for storage. The deepfreeze is best for long time storage.

ONIONS

Choose onions with strong aroma and flavor. Sweet Spanish, White Portugal, and Southport Globe are a few varieties. Peak harvest time is August through January.

Choose firm dry onions that have an outer bright, smooth skin that rustles when it is touched. Avoid sprouting onions, and watch for dampness or softness at the stem end.

Prepare: Remove the outside skin of the onion. Wash in cold water, dry on terry towel, and place in deepfreeze for 10 minutes before chopping. This helps avoid tears when preparing the onions. A Veg-o-matic is useful for preparing them. An onion may be felled with one quick blow on the Veg-o-matic. Some blenders have a chop speed that will prepare the onions, or mixers have vegetable slicers; and if these conveniences aren't available, watch the galloping gourmet to learn the tricks from him. Place the prepared onion on the tray and dry.

Puree onions to make leather. Dry crisp, remove from the plastic wrap, powder in the blender, and mix with salt for onion salt; or use plain as powdered onion. One tablespoon of onion powder is equal to 1 medium sized onion. One tablespoon of minced onion soaked in 1 tablespoon of water for 5 minutes is equal to 1 medium-sized onion chopped.

PAPAYA

Most papayas come from Hawaii by air.

The peak season for papaya is May and June. Choose a papaya which is pale green with speckled yellow starting at the blossom end. The papaya should have a smooth skin without bruises or dark spots. It will finish ripening if left at room temperature. Do not use in gelatin salad unless it has been steamed.

Prepare: Wash carefully, cut in half, scoop out the seeds, peel, slice in 3/8-inch slices, dip into ascorbic acid, drain in colander, place on net on the tray, and dehydrate.

Papaya Cheese Tart

1 cup dehydrated slices of papaya	1 cup dehydrated pineapple chunks
1-1/2 cups of water (to rehydrate above)	2 bananas, sliced
1 unbaked 8-inch pie shell	1/4 cup lime juice
6 Tbsp granulated sugar	1 package (8 ounces) cream cheese, softened
1 egg	1/2 tsp vanilla
1/2 cup whipping cream	1 Tbsp date sugar

In medium bowl, combine papaya, pineapple, water, and lime juice. Marinate several hours, stirring occasionally. Using a fork, prick pie shell in several places; bake at 425° F. 10 minutes. Meanwhile, beat together cream cheese, granulated sugar, egg, and vanilla. Remove pie shell from oven and lower oven temperature to 350° F. Pour the cheese mixture into the crust. Return to the oven to bake 10 minutes more. Cool. To serve, whip cream, and add date sugar. Add bananas to fruit, and pile onto cheese filling. Garnish with whipped cream and strawberries, if desired.

PARSLEY

This herb is rich in calcium, niacin, vitamin A and vitamin C. Parsley should be harvested regularly when grown in home gardens. The larger outer leaves should be cut or broken first. Always cut or break close to the core of the plant. Do not leave parts of the stem attached. The whole plant can be harvested, but care should be taken to cut it about 1 inch above the ground so as not to damage the growing point.

Prepare: Do not use yellow or wilted sprigs. Wash carefully, drain on absorbent towel, place on net on trays, and dehydrate. Separate the leaf bunches from the main stem. Discard the stem and dry the leaves.

Parsley is good used for a seasoning after it has been dehydrated, but it is not recommended for use as a garnish.

PEACHES

There are so many different varieties available that it is prohibitive to mention all of them. Elberta is one of the oldest varieties. Lovell and Rio Oso Gem Peaches are supposed to be good dehydrating peaches because they have less moisture content.

This is another fruit that must be picked mature or it will be flavorless. Avoid greenish fruit. It will not ripen. Soft, split or bruised (cut out bruises or they will taste) fruit may be used for leather, but use only firm yellowish background fruit for slices. Those varieties with deep-red centers will have a dark center when dehydrated. For eye appeal in wet-pack this is desirable, but for dehydrating it can look unappetizing. Purchase peaches medium to large. Avoid small misshapen peaches. A sign of overripe or injured peaches is mold (the kind that grows on bread). If the fruit fly is hovering over the lug, it is a sign of decaying fruit. One side of a peach should have a green background color that will change to yellow when fully ripe, and the other side should be rosy. The peak harvest season is from July through the middle of September.

Prepare: Scald, for more easy removal of skins, or peel, cut in half, remove stone, cut each half in 3/8-inch slices, put into ascorbic acid, drain in colander, place on net on tray, and dehydrate.

Peaches are delicious in cobblers, ice cream, pies, sauce served over angel food cake, snack foods, etc.

PEARS

Two good varieties are Bartlett and Bosc. The latter is known in the West as the Russet pear because of its russet coloring.

Pears have to be picked when mature, but they will still be hard and green. They do not ripen successfully on the tree. They will have better flavor without mealiness if they are kept at a temperature below 70° F. for home ripening. Avoid pears with cuts, bruises, or dark spots. The Bartlett pear will change from light green to yellow when it is ready to prepare. The Bosc will also be yellow, but the russet coloring will stand out.

Prepare: Carefully wash, peel, cut in quarters, remove core and cut each quarter into 3 or 4 slices depending on the size of the pear. Do not soak pears in salt water because the water-soluble nutrients will be lost. Prepare only 3 or 4 pears at a time and place them in ascorbic acid. Coat well, place in colander to drain and do 3 or 4 more pears. Work quickly to preserve nutrients and color. Fill one tray at a time and put it immediately into the preheated dehydrator. Place pears on net to dry.

Dried Fruit Bread

4 cups assorted dried fruits
   (apples, apricots, peaches,
   pears, raisins, persimmons)
1 cup apple juice
2 Tbsp active dry yeast
2 cups warm water
1/4 cup honey
1/4 cup brown sugar
2 tsp salt
1 tsp cinnamon

1 Tbsp anise seed
1/2 tsp ground cloves
1/2 cup wheat germ
1/2 cup margarine, melted
About 7 cups unsifted flour
1 cup pitted and chopped
   dates
1/2 cup each, chopped
   almonds and walnuts

Cut fruits into 1/4-inch pieces. Heat apple juice to just under boiling point, add cut fruits and set aside to rehydrate. In the large bowl of a bread mixer, soften yeast in 1/2 cup of warm water (110° F.) for 5 minutes. Add 1-1/2 cups warm water, honey, brown sugar, salt, anise, cloves, cinnamon, wheat germ, and melted margarine. Gradually add 3-1/2 cups of flour and mix at medium speed for 5 minutes. Add 1-1/2 cups of flour. Add flour until consistency is correct for kneading by machine (about 2 cups).

Knead for 5 minutes. Remove from mixer, place in greased bowl, turn to grease top, cover, and let rise until doubled (1-1/2 hours). Add dates and nuts to the fruit mixture. Place half of the dough on a lightly-floured board. Flatten to a 1/2-inch thick circle. Place half of the fruit mixture on top and gradually work it throughout the dough, adding only enough flour to prevent it from sticking. Flatten the remaining dough and repeat. Place in two well-greased 5 x 9-inch loaf pans, cover lightly, and let rise in a warm place until doubled (1 hour). Brush loaves with melted butter. Bake in a 350° F. oven until the bread pulls away from the sides of the pan (1 hour). If it browns too fast, cover lightly with foil. Remove from pans, cool on racks before placing in plastic bags for storage.

Wrinkled Fruit Squares

1 cup well-packed dehy-
  drated fruit pieces
  (peaches, prunes, pears,
  apples, bananas, etc. or a
  combination) rehydrated in
3/4 cup boiling water (Let
  stand for 10 minutes, then
  drain and save water.)
1/2 cup Safflower oil
1 egg

1/2 tsp baking soda dis-
  solved in water drained
  from fruit
1/2 tsp each of the following: cinnamon, salt,
  nutmeg, and cloves
1 cup oatmeal
1 cup flour
1/2 cup granulated sugar
1/2 cup brown sugar

Add baking soda to water drained from fruit. Combine all ingredients. Mix well. Nuts may be added if desired. Spread evenly in a well-greased 13 x 9 inch pan. Bake at 350° F. for 20 minutes. Cool and cut into squares. The batter may also be used as drop cookies.

PEAS

When planting peas, choose varieties of seed that are wrinkled. The peas will be sweeter than smooth seeded varieties.

Look for shiny, bright green pods with young tender sweet peas. Avoid peas filled completely, especially if the pod is turning white. These peas would be tough because the sugar is turning to starch. The peak season for peas is June through August.

Prepare: Shell peas, steam blanch until they just begin to shrivel, plunge into cold water, drain on terry towel, place on net on tray and dehydrate.

Hamburger Soup

Place the following ingredients into a large kettle:

1/2 cup dehydrated onion	1/2 cup dehydrated green
1 cup dehydrated carrots	beans
1 cup dehydrated peas	1/2 cup dehydrated corn
1/2 cup dehydrated celery	1/2 cup dehydrated
tops	zucchini
2 cups dehydrated tomatoes	1 cup dehydrated potatoes

To rehydrate the vegetables, cover with boiling water. Let them stand for 5 minutes to absorb the water. While waiting, brown 1 pound of hamburger and drain. Add the hamburger and 9 cups of water to the vegetables. Let the soup simmer slowly for 10 minutes. Add 5 peppercorns, 3 tablespoons of beef base or 3 bouillon cubes, and simmer until the vegetables are tender and the seasoning has been absorbed. Serve. Individual taste determines the amount of water to add. If a lot of broth is desirable, then more water needs to be added to this recipe.

Note: Noodles, alphabet macaroni or dumplings may be added, if desired.

PEPPERS

Peppers are classed in two groups, the sweet or mild and the hot. California Wonder and Burpee's Tasty Hybrid are good varieties in the bell pepper. Long Red Cayenne and Jalapeno are two varieties of hot chili peppers. The Long Red Cayenne is easily dried.

Both sweet and hot peppers are produced in abundance in August and September. Look for firm, dark green peppers and avoid black spots. A red bell pepper is not a different variety, but a green pepper that is sweet and fully ripened. Avoid dull looking chilies. Always wear rubber gloves when preparing hot peppers.

Prepare: Wash, clean out the seeds and dice in 1/4-inch cubes to be used in casseroles. It is not necessary to blanch diced peppers. Place them on net on a tray and dry.

Chilies should be washed and dried whole. The drying time will be decreased if they are halved.

PERSIMMONS

You can tell the variety by taste test when the fruit is firm. If the fruit is firm and the mouth puckers, then it must be a

Hachiya, and if there is no puckering, it must be a Fuyu. Fuyu are smaller and can be eaten while still firm.

Persimmons are "in season" during October and November. They are very perishable. The coloring is beautiful. They are a deep orange-red. The persimmon gets its color before it is ripe so always be sure to choose a soft one for eating to avoid the puckery taste.

Prepare: Remove stem cap, wash carefully, cut in half and then slice into 3/8-inch slices. To help retain the vitamin A and C, it should be coated with ascorbic acid, drained, and placed on net to dry.

Persimmon Bread

Mix:

3 cups sugar	1-1/2 tsp salt
1 cup oil	1 tsp each of cinnamon,
4 eggs	nutmeg and cloves

Add:

2 tsp soda, dissolved in 1/2 cup water	3-1/2 cups of flour
1 well-packed cup of dehydrated persimmons reconstituted for 5 minutes in 1-1/2 cups of boiling water. (Blend in blender.)	Nuts or raisins may be added if desired

Bake in two greased 9 x 5-inch loaf pans at 350° F. for 1 hour or until it tests done. Remove from pans at once and cool on rack.

PINEAPPLE

The two most common varieties are Smooth Cayenne (so named because of its smooth-edged leaves) and Red Spanish (the crown leaves have sawteeth along the edge).

Starch is stored in the stem of the pineapple plant. Just before the fruit matures, the starch is changed to sugar and is transferred from the stem to the fruit. If the fruit is picked before ripening takes place, it will not be sweet. When markets advertise fast shipment of mature fruit, try one to see the difference.

The outside color of the pineapple should be yellow to orange with a golden-colored meat inside. Buying larger pineapples increases the amount of edible fruit. The core remains about the same size and the rind is the same thickness regardless of weight. Therefore, it is more economical to buy a large pineapple.

The price of pineapple stays quite steady all year, but the prime time of purchase is late March through June.

When choosing a pineapple, avoid greenish fruits with bruises, soft spots, dull color, or dried out leaves. A pineapple is sweeter at the base and more acid at the crown.

Prepare: Slice in quarters from top to bottom. Remove the meat from the rind (similar to preparing cantaloupe), and cut into tidbit size pieces. For long time storage, coat with ascorbic acid, drain, place on net on tray, and dehydrate. If pineapple tidbits are to be used in a set gelatin salad, it will be necessary to steam blanch instead of coating with ascorbic acid.

When preparing more than two pineapples at one time, it is wise to wear rubber gloves to protect hands.

PLUMS AND PRUNES

Prunes are oval, small, deep-purple or dark-blue, with greenish yellow to light-amber flesh, and a firm, meaty texture which is sweet, tart, and subacid. Plums are oval and round, large, green, yellow rod, or blue (unstable in color), with green, yellow-red, or pinkish flesh, and a soft and juicy texture.

Plum describes those fruits eaten fresh and canned. Plums will not dehydrate without removing the stone. Prunes are the varieties that can be dehydrated without removing the stone. Stanley is a freestone prune-type plum. Italian prune plums make good-flavored prunes. The prime season for plums and prunes is June through August.

Prepare: *Plums*—Wash, remove stone, slice in 1/4-inch slices, and place on net on trays to dehydrate.

Prunes—Wash, dip into boiling water for 60 seconds, plunge into ice water to stop cooking action, dry on absorbent towel, and place on net on tray to dehydrate.

POTATOES

The Russett Burbank and White Rose are good dehydrating varieties.

New potatoes have a low starch content, and will dehydrate better than mature potatoes. Potatoes are sold as "special items" in the fall and in the spring before the new crop of potatoes come to market. They can be dehyrated for hash browns, and potato panckaes. Because of better transportation and extended harvest, there is really no peak season for potatoes.

Avoid potatoes with a greenish cast. They have been exposed to light too long and will be bitter. Do not buy potatoes that are sprouting.

Prepare: Scrub new potatoes with a vegetable brush, slice in 1/4-inch rounds, steam blanch until they are tender or translucent, quickly immerse in ice water to stop cooking action, drain on absorbent towel, place in dehydrator on net on trays and dry.

For mature potatoes, scrub thoroughly, pare, slice in 1/4-inch rounds, cut french fry style, or grate, wash the potatoes again, and steam for about 5 minutes, or until the potato is translucent. Plunge into cold water to stop cooking action, drain on absorbent towel, place on net on tray, and dry.

When starch foods such as potatoes are cooked, the starch granules swell and absorb water (steam). Starch does not dissolve in water; therefore the potatoes, after being steamed, become pasty. The smaller the potatoes are cut for dehydrating the greater the problem is with the stickiness.

Grated potatoes are really quite pasty during preparation for dehydration. When they are dehydrated, they have a starchy glazed coating. After reconstitution, they are just like fresh grated potatoes. The starchy glaze is reabsorbed into the potato. It is a little harder to get the grated potato steamed properly, but with care, it can be done. Do not overcrowd the steamer. After dehydrating, it is obvious which potatoes did not get steamed. They are black! The flavor is fine, but they do not look too appetizing.

Note: Potato granules require a spray-dry process for quality mashed potatoes.

Quick Escalloped Potatoes

3 cups of rehydrated grated potatoes (use 1-1/2 cups of boiling water, cover the potatoes and let them stand for about 5 minutes).

Layer half of the potatoes in a well-buttered 9 x 9-inch baking dish. Put a layer of Mozzarella cheese on top of the potatoes, sprinkle with minced ham TVP, and put remaining potatoes on top. Season 1 cup of milk with salt, white pepper, and 1 tablespoon of dehydrated onions. Pour this over the ingredients in the casserole. If the potatoes are not covered, add enough milk to cover. Place several squares of butter on top. Bake at 350° F. until tender

Sliced potatoes may be used, but it will take longer for them to cook.

PUMPKIN

The variety doesn't matter so long as it ends up in a pie! For purchasing, the best buy is after Halloween. Pumpkins store well if they are kept in a cool place.

The reason for dehydrating pumpkin is to preserve the remainder of the Jack-O'-Lantern. To children, carving is fun, but pie eating is also a very important event.

Prepare: Peel, steam, cool, puree, place on plastic wrap, and dry like leather. After being reconstituted, the pumpkin is good when it is used for pies, cookies, pumpkin ice cream, leather, and bread.

Pumpkin Leather

2 cups pumpkin pureed   2 Tbsp honey
1/2 tsp pumpkin pie spice

Blend above ingredients together, and pour onto plastic wrap to dry. This makes 1 cup of broken pieces. When it is reconstituted with 1-1/2 cups of water, it can be used to flavor ice cream, shakes, cookies, or pumkin bread. Pour the water over the pumpkin pieces and let them soak for 5 minutes. Put the ingredients into the blender and puree. This amount is equal to 2 cups of pumpkin.

Don't throw those pumpkin seeds away! Scoop them out, wash them lightly with water to separate them from the fibre, and spread them on net on the dryer trays to dry. After they have been dried, they can be sprouted or toasted.

Roasted Pumpkin Seeds

Use 1 tablespoon of melted margarine for each 2 cups of seeds. Spread out in a single layer in a shallow baking pan or on a cookie sheet, sprinkle with salt, and roast at 250° F. for about 1/2 hour—until the seeds are lightly browned. Stir occasionally while roasting. Spread seeds onto a paper towel, and let them cool.

Quick Preparation: Heat 1 tablespoon of cooking oil in a frying pan, add seeds, and stir gently. Some seeds will "pop", so have a lid handy. The seeds will swell in a few seconds. Remove them from the heat at once, dry on absorbent paper, season with salt, and eat.

RASPBERRIES

For home planting choose an everbearing variety like Heritage. Latham is a good fresh or preserving berry.

The raspberry season starts in May, with the peak season in June and July. Red raspberries are very delicate. They should look fresh, clean, and have a uniform bright-red color. Overripe berries are dull, dark-red, and soft. When raspberries are ripe, they separate from the cap. Avoid berries with caps. Do not wash fruits until just before dehydrating.

Prepare: Wash, dip into ascorbic acid, drain, place on net on tray, and dry. Raspberries are good used in shakes, ice cream, syrups, toppings, on cereal, and in pies. Make the same as the recipe for strawberry pie except substitute raspberries.

RHUBARB

Rhubarb may be planted from seed or roots. Some good varieties are MacDonald, Valentine, and Victoria. With hothouse cultivation, rhubarb has now become available year around.

Most field crops of rhubarb are harvested in April and May. If the rhubarb is grown in the home-garden it can be harvested from April through October. The leaves of rhubarb contain oxalic acid, and should be discarded. Do not harvest more than two-thirds of any plants stalks at one time. To gather, remove the larger outside stalks, grasp them firmly near the base, and quickly pull from the crown. The stalks will separate at ground level, and allow the plant to continue to produce. *Do not* cut the stalks.

If purchasing rhubarb, look for firm, straight, crisp stalks. Keep rhubarb under refrigeration until time of preparation. Red stalked rhubarb is sweeter than other varieties.

Prepare: Trim, wash, slice crosswise into 3/8-inch slices, and place on netting on trays to dry.

Rhubarb Punch

Place 3 cups of dehydrated rhubarb into a pan with 3 cups of water and simmer for 5 minutes. Cool, and puree in the blender.

Add:

1 12-ounce can of frozen orange juice plus water	1 12-ounce can of frozen lemonade plus water
1 cup sugar	1 quart gingerale

Rhubarb is good mixed with strawberries for tarts and pies.

SAGE

There are more than a dozen varieties of sage. The most popular plant has a squarish stem with rounded-oblong leaves on short stems. Purple flowers appear in August at the upper end of the plant. The leaves have a silvery cast. Sage thrives best in a well-aerated soil. Sage will survive even hard winters if the last harvest is taken no later than September, and only the leaves and stems high up on the plant are picked.

Prepare: Pick the leaves, wash carefully, dry on absorbent towel, place on trays in dehydrator. Do not turn the heating element on, but let it dry with just the fans movement of air. Store the leaves whole.

Sage Sauce

1 tsp of finely chopped dehydrated onion	1/2 tsp of finely rubbed sage leaves
1/4 cup of water	Simmer gently for 10 min.

Add:

1 tsp salt	1 Tbsp of fine bread-
1/4 tsp fresh ground pepper	crumbs

Mix well and pour into 1 cup of broth, gravy, or melted butter. Simmer a few minutes longer. Serve this sauce with roast pork, duck, or green peas.

SPROUTS

If too many sprouts are grown, it is possible to dry them, grind them in a herb grinder and use them as seasonings.

Prepare: Alfalfa, Fenugreek, Chia, etc. can be placed on a tray to dry. When they are dry, blend them in the blender to make a seasoning to sprinkle over the tops of casseroles, stews, omelets, etc. Do not blend or grind them until they are ready to be used. Do not turn on heating element.

STRAWBERRIES

The Marshall keeps a good color and doesn't turn dark when combined with sugar in jam-making; therefore, it should be a good variety to dry. Strawberries have a high vitamin C content and should be treated with ascorbic acid to help retain the vitamin C.

Look for bright-red colored, plump berries with caps and solid color. Berries with white tips indicate unripened fruit. By placing them in the sun, they may turn red, but they will not have the natural sugar and flavor of vine-ripened fruit. Berries are available from May through August at reasonable prices.

Berries are sold by the flat. Each flat should contain 12 baskets averaging 15 ounces each. Sometimes markets repackage flats into 12-ounce cups and make an extra 2-1/2 to 3 cups per flat. Check the quality, weights and prices to select the best buy.

Prepare: Remove the cap, wash gently, slice vertically (for eye appeal) into 3/8-inch slices, dip into ascorbic acid solution, drain, place on net and dehydrate. Ascorbic acid helps retain vitamin C and also keeps the color more appetizing.

Strawberries are delicious with granola for breakfast. They also make good shakes, ice cream and strawberry pie.

STRAWBERRY PIE

Heat 1-7/8 cups of water to boiling. Never use milk. Add 1 cup of cold water to 5 ounces of Junket Danish Dessert and Pie Filling (Currant-Raspberry-Strawberry if it is available). Mix well, stirring until the mixture is smooth. Add the mixture to the boiling water, stirring constantly, until it boils. Remove from the heat, and stir in 1-1/2 cups of dehydrated strawberries which have been reconstituted in 3/4 of a cup of boiling water for 5 minutes. Add 1/4 cup of sugar to berries just before mixing them into the junket. Pour the mixture into a baked 9" pastry shell, a graham cracker crust, or individual tart shells. Sprinkle the surface lightly with sugar while it is warm to keep the surface moist. Refrigerate for 3 hours before serving. Garnish with whipped cream just before serving.

SQUASH

Summer varieties—Crookneck, Zucchini, Italian and Scallop. Winter varieties—Hubbard and Banana. Summer squash are at their peak from June through August.

Summer squash have soft skins and are recommended for dehydrating. Winter squash store so well it is not necessary to dry them. If the squash is so large that it may spoil before it can be eaten, then it is wise to dehydrate the excess.

For best quality, use summer squash while they are young and tender. Generally a summer squash is too old for good eating (therefore drying) when the thumbnail does not easily pierce the skin without pressure. Of course there is always an exception. Zucchini for bread can be more mature because it will be grated.

Prepare: Is it necessary to steam summer squash? It is a matter of opinion. The decision remains with the individual. To some people if they are not steamed before being dehydrated, they are tough. To other people if they are steamed before being dehydrated, they are mushy. Try some both ways to find individual preference. Wash the squash thoroughly, cut it into 3/8-inch slices and place on net on trays to dry. Make some slices less than 1/4-inch thick to be dehydrated crisp for chips for dips. Grate some to rehydrate for zucchini bread. For dips, the small squash without seeds is best.

When steaming summer squash, only steam for 2 minutes. Stop the cooking action by placing in ice water. Drain on absorbent towel and place on netting to dry.

Winter squash should be steamed until it is tender, cooled in ice water, drained on absorbent towel and placed on net to dry. It may also be pureed in the blender, poured as leather and used as mashed squash for a vegetable dish.

ZUCCHINI BREAD

3 eggs
2 cups sugar
2 cups grated zucchini
  (1-1/2 cups boiling
  water and 1 heaping
  cup of dehydrated
  zucchini)
1/2 tsp baking powder

3 tsp cinnamon
1 cup oil
2 tsp vanilla
3 cups flour
1 tsp soda
1 tsp salt
1/2 cup chopped nuts

Beat eggs until they are light and foamy. Add oil, sugar, zucchini and vanilla. Mix lightly, but well. Mix flour, soda, baking powder, salt, and cinnamon in a bowl. Add the flour mixture to the first mixture and blend. Add nuts. Bake in two greased 9 x 5-inch loaf pans at 325° F. for 1 hour. Remove from pans and cool.

SWEET POTATOES OR YAMS

Yams are "in season" from November to March. Sweet potatoes are available beginning in September through April.

Sweet potatoes are light yellowish-tan tubers with light yellow or pale orange inside meat. Choose a small to medium-sized sweet potato, well-shaped, smooth skinned and firm. Avoid growth cracks, damp areas, shriveled and discolored potatoes.

Yams are brownish colored with a deep-orange flesh. They are sweeter and more moist than sweet potatoes. Choose them just as sweet potatoes are chosen.

Prepare: Scrub well, steam until tender, cool in ice water, place on absorbent toweling to dry, remove peeling (if desired), slice in 3/8-inch slices, place on net on trays and dry. They may also be dried as leather to make sweet potato pies. It takes about 5 minutes for yams or sweet potatoes to become translucent.

CANDIED SWEET POTATOES

Place 1-1/2 cups of sweet potatoes or yams in a pan. Cover with 1-1/2 cups of pineapple juice. Simmer until reconstituted. Place in a 9 x 9-inch square baking dish. Add 1/2 cup dehydrated pineapple tidbits, 2 tablespoons brown sugar or date sugar and cover top with miniature marshmallows. Place in a 350° F. oven until marshmallows are toasted. Serves 4.

THYME

Thyme requires full sun and a sandy, dry soil. The small oval-shaped leaves are attached to woody stems and branches. Leaves are grey-green and lavender flowers appear at the tip ends in May. Honey bees are attracted by the flowers. Harvest thyme just before the flowers begin to open by cutting the plant two inches from the ground. Only one cutting should be made to protect the plant in cold winter climates.

Prepare: After cutting the plant, wash carefully, lay on absorbent toweling to remove as much moisture as possible, place on dehydrator tray and dry. Do not turn the heating element on, but use only the fan. The leaves will separate from the woody stems with slight rubbing when they are dry. The leaves alone are usable. Store leaves in a dark, dry place.

TOMATOES

Variety isn't as important as having a tomato selected for the soil and area in which it is to be grown. Look for firm, red tomatoes. Avoid split, soft tomatoes. Low acid tomatoes will turn black when they are dehydrated, therefore, pretreatment is necessary.

Prepare: Remove stems, wash, scald in boiling water to loosen skins, chill in cold water, peel, cut into quarters. If tomatoes are cut into 1/2-inch wedges and placed with the wedge side on the net, the nutrients will accumulate on the top side of the wedge instead of running onto the tray. They can also be cut into 3/8-inch rounds. They look pretty this way, but are not quite as nutritious. Cherry tomatoes may be cut in half and dried with skin side down. Tomato skins are tough when dehydrated. Steam blanch low-acid tomatoes for 2-3 minutes to prevent discoloration. To prevent darkening of fruit leather, add 1 tablespoon of vinegar or 2 teaspoons of lemon juice per quart; or boil puree for 2 minutes and cool.

Tomato-vegetable leather can be made by placing tomatoes, cucumbers, onion, pepper and celery in the blender. Puree and place on plastic wrap to dry. After it has dried crisp, put it back into the blender and make a powder to be used as tomato paste, sauce, or juice; depending on the amount of water used to reconstitute it. Pour less than 1/4-inch thick for quicker drying. Reconstitute with 1 tablespoon per 1/4—1/2—1 cup. Dehydrated tomatoes are very strong-flavored because of the loss of moisture. Therefore, they are too strong as a snack food to be appetizing to most people.

Tomatoes taste like freshly picked, rather than canned tomatoes when they are reconstituted. They are too soft to be used in salads; but are delicious in stews, casseroles, or any dish where cooked tomatoes can be used.

TURKEY

Use dehydrated left-over turkey for turkey a la king, turkey pot pie, sour cream chip dip, etc.

Prepare: Cut cold turkey into quarter-inch thick slices of convenient lengths, depending on use. Place on net on tray and dehydrate.

Small pieces of dehydrated turkey, dropped into sour cream for chip dips will absorb sufficient moisture from the sour cream to make them the right consistency to serve.

Quarter-inch cubes of turkey are a good size to make good turkey a la king or pot pie. Just add equal parts of boiling water and turkey to your favorite recipe. Long strips make a crisp, munchy, snack-food.

Be sure to cut all fat off from the turkey. It is very unappetizing to bite into cold fat. It trims more easily when the turkey is cold.

YOGURT

Check the temperature of the dehydrator with a thermometer. It should not go over 120° F. or below 105° F. It takes 8 to 10 hours to make yogurt in a commercial yogurt maker. It can be made in 5 hours in the dehydrator.

Yogurt—Fresh Milk

4 cups milk
1 heaping Tbsp yogurt
(unflavored)

1/2 cup instant
powdered milk

Add powdered milk to milk and heat to boiling for a few seconds. Cool to 120° F. Add 1 heaping tablespoon of yogurt (plain) with 1/4 cup of the boiled milk to make a thick sauce. Add this to the remainder of the milk. Stir well. Empty the mixture into clean glass jars with lids and place on the fifth shelf of the dehydrator (middle). Check after 5 hours to see if it is set. If it is, cool immediately. If it is not set, check it every 20 minutes until it sets.

Dehydrated fruit for flavoring is best added just prior to cooling. The fruit absorbs the yogurt moisture and makes a good thick yogurt.

Yogurt—Powdered Milk

2-2/3 cups water (120° F.)	1 heaping Tbsp unflavored
1 scant cup of non-instant	yogurt
powdered milk	

Pour water into a blender. Turn on at low speed; add the powdered milk slowly and blend until smooth. Add the yogurt and blend a few seconds. Place in jars in dehydrator. Chill immediately when set.

Tips for Beginners:

1. Use plain commercial yogurt for a start or use yogurt from the last batch (shouldn't be more than a week old).

2. Do not disturb or stir the yogurt while it is setting.

3. If temperature is too hot (over 120° F.), it will kill yogurt bacteria. If the temperature is too cool (below 100° F.), ordinary sour milk bacteria develop.

4. If yogurt is bubbly and starts to separate, it has been in the dehydrator too long. After 5 hours check to see if the yogurt is set; recheck the yogurt every 20 minutes until it is set.

5. The more you stir yogurt, the thinner it becomes. Fold flavoring lightly into the yogurt to prevent thinning.

6. Yogurt will keep in the refrigerator for about 1 week. Make it at least once a week to keep a fresh starter.

7. The longer yogurt sets in the refrigerator the more pronounced the flavor.

8. Use powdered sugar to sweeten the yogurt and prevent graininess.

Uses for Yogurt:

Add individually preferred herbs and spices for gourmet dressings.

Use fresh, canned, dried, or strained fruit in plain yogurt.

Use concentrated juices (frozen) to flavor yogurt.

Use yogurt as a substitute for sour cream in chip dips, baked potato dressing, cream sauces, etc.

When adding dried fruit to yogurt, add it after the yogurt comes from the dehydrator and before it is chilled. The dried fruit absorbs moisture from the yogurt resulting in a thicker yogurt.

Use yogurt as a substitute for buttermilk—1 cup of yogurt plus 1 cup of water, equals 2 cups of buttermilk.

Add 1 cup of yogurt to a 3 ounce package of partially set jello. Leave out 1/4 cup of the recommended water when setting the jello. Lime, orange, lemon, and berry jello may be used. Individual taste determines a favorite.

Frozen berry jams, or cooked jams make good flavorings for yogurt. Just add about 1 tablespoonful to a 5 ounce jar of yogurt.

Rosie's Refresher

1/2 cup orange juice	2 Tbsp brown sugar
1/2 cup yogurt	1 scoop vanilla ice cream
1/2 cup water	

Blend in blender. Makes 2 tall glasses.

Yogurt Tea Cake

2 cups flour	1 cube margarine
1 tsp baking soda	1 cup brown sugar
1/2 tsp baking powder	1 egg
1/4 tsp salt	1 tsp vanilla
1 cup yogurt	1 Tbsp jam

Beat margarine and sugar until creamy and then add egg and vanilla. Stir in flour mixture alternately with yogurt and jam, just until blended. Spoon into greased tube mold or angel cake pan. Bake at 350° F. for 50 minutes. Cool in pan on wire rack for 10 minutes. Loosen carefully around the edge and turn out onto a rack to cool completely. Just before serving, sprinkle with powdered sugar.

Yogurt Dessert Cake

5 large eggs	1 tsp vanilla
2 cups yogurt flavored with	3/4 tsp salt
1/4 cup of dehydrated	1/2 tsp grated lemon
berries, peaches, or	peel
persimmons, etc.	powdered sugar (optional)
1/2 cup honey	

Separate 2 eggs. Set aside the whites for the meringue and use 1 yolk for the butter crust. Combine 3 whole eggs and 1 yolk in a large mixing bowl. Reserve.

Prepare butter crust.

Butter Crust

1 cup sifted flour	2 Tbsp sugar
1/4 tsp salt	1/4 cup softened butter
1 egg yolk	or margarine

Resift flour with sugar and salt, and add butter and egg yolk. Use hands to mix well. The mixture will be crumbly. Pat the mixture evenly over the bottom and 1/2-inch up the sides of a 9-inch springform pan.

Beat the whole egg mixture well and brush the inside of the unbaked crust thoroughly. Bake at 400° F. for 15 minutes.

To the remaining egg mixture, add the yogurt, 4 tablespoons of honey, vanilla, salt and lemon peel. Beat well. With clean beaters, beat egg whites to soft peaks. Beat in the remaining 2 tablespoons of honey and continue beating to a soft meringue. Fold gently into yogurt mixture. Set the oven temperature to 350° F. Pour the filling into the pre-baked crust and bake for about 40 minutes— just until it is set. Cool thoroughly before cutting. Sift powdered sugar lightly over the top before serving. This makes 1 (9-inch) cake.

CHAPTER XV

THE SYNOPSIS

Dehydration is a new concept of home food preparation and storage. Dehydration is an economical way to preserve fruits, vegetables, meats, poultry, and fish.

After learning the processes and techniques, many people can make nutritious convenience foods and snacks and have fun doing it. Dehydration builds a new vocabulary: enzymes, pH factor, case hardening, high humidity, pretreatment, erythorbic acid, invert sugars, sodium bisulfite, and other terms all play an important role in the process of preparing nutritional foods by dehydration.

With helpful hints and preparation guides it is easy to save time, money, and space by dehydrating food for storage, backpacking, boating, camping, snacking, hiking, flying, etc.

Dehydrated food can be rehydrated and used in the place of fresh food in the favorite recipes of the family. There are new and interesting recipes to try using rehydrated food, but family favorite recipes should not be put aside. Rehydrated food can be used in the place of fresh food, frozen food, and canned food.

FOOD DEHYDRATION TERMINOLOGY

Absorption — To take up water—a soaking up.

Antioxidant — A substance that prevents or delays oxidation.

Ascorbic Acid — A water-soluble vitamin known as vitamin C.

Bacteria — Tiny, one-celled organisms, visible only under a microscope, which are widely distributed in the air, water, soil, and animal and plant tissues. Many bacteria cause harmful spoilage of foods.

Blanching — To preheat in boiling water or steam. Blanching is used to inactivate enzymes and to aid in the removal of skins from fruits and vegetables.

Carotene — Yellow plant pigments occurring abundantly in dark-green leafy and deep-yellow vegetables. Alpha, beta, and gamma carotenes are provitamins which may be converted into vitamin A in the body.

Case Hardening — If the temperature is too high and too much air is blowing over the product being dehydrated, the outside layer hardens and traps the moisture inside. This condition extends the drying time and may even cause spoilage.

Checking — To craze the skin of wax-coated fruits by dipping into boiling water to facilitate the movement of the center moisture to the outside.

Dehydration — To become relatively free from water. The process of preserving food by removing water, and also reducing bulk and weight.

Dehydrofreezing — A relatively new process which consists of evaporating about half of the water from fruits and vegetables and then freezing the product.

Drying — The process of removing the moisture in foods which is capable of bringing about the decomposition of the food.

Enzyme — An organic compound of protein nature produced by living tissue to accelerate metabolic reactions.

Fat-Soluble — Refers to substances that cannot be dissolved in water but can be dissolved in fats.

Flat-Sour — Souring of products being dehydrated because of overcrowding the trays, high temperatures, lack of air movement, and improper pretreatment.

Food Preservation — To protect food from contamination and to maintain its color, flavor, texture, and nutritive value.

Inactivate — To render inactive, to destroy certain biological activities and stop enzyme action.

Jerky — Meat cut in long slices or strips and dried.

Leaching — The loss of water-soluble minerals and vitamins by soaking, steaming, or boiling of vegetables and fruits.

Leather — Pureed fruits or berries, spread in layers on plastic wrap, and dehydrated.

Nutrients — An organic or inorganic substance in food which is digested and absorbed in the gastrointestinal tract and utilized in metabolism.

Nylon Net — An extra heavy-duty, fine mesh, netting material used on dryer trays for easy removal of food.

Oxidation — A chemical process by which a substance combines with oxygen.

Plastic Wrap — Any good grade of food safe plastic material that can be cut to dehydrator shelf size to hold leathers, cookies, granola, etc.

Pretreat — To exercise care in processing food to retain a high nutritional value.

Provitamin — The forerunner of a vitamin—provitamin A is carotene.

Puree — A smooth, pulpy food product from which rough fiber has been removed by sieving or blending.

Reconstitute — To restore to the normal state, usually by adding water. Unsalted broth or juice may also be used.

Rehydration — Soaking or cooking or using other procedures to make dehydrated foods take up the water they lost during drying.

Simmer — To cook in liquid just below boiling point on the top of the stove.

Sulfuring — This is a process where pure sulfur is burned, exposing the fruit to the fumes in order to prevent browning, to help repel insects, and to speed up drying time.

Vitamin — Organic compound occurring in minute amounts in foods and essential for life and growth.

Water-Soluble — Refers generally to substances that dissolve in water—vitamins and minerals.

METRIC CONVERSION EQUIVALENTS

For best results, use standard measuring spoons and cups with all measurements level.*

1 teaspoon (tsp.)	= 1/6 fl. oz., or 5 cc
1 tablespoon (tbsp.)	= 1/2 fl. oz., or 15 cc
1 fluid ounce (fl. oz.)	= 29.6 cc
1 measuring cup (c.)	= 237 cc or 8 fl. oz.
1 quart (2 pints, 4 cups)	= 947 cc
1 pound (lb.)	= 454 Gm
1 ounce (avoirdupois)	= 28.3 Gm
1 kilogram (kg)	= 2.2 lb.
1 liter	= 1.057 qt.
100 cubic centimeter (cc)	= 3 1/3 fl. oz.

*Values are slightly rounded off to give workable figures.

BUYING GUIDE
Approximate Yield per Pound

Fresh Produce

Apples = 3 medium; 2 3/4 cups sliced
Apricots = 8-12 medium; 2 1/2 cups halved
Asparagus = 2 cups, cooked
Bananas = 3 medium; 1 1/3 cups, mashed
Beans, green = 3 cups, cooked
Carrots = 2 cups, cooked
Lemons = 4 medium; 2/3 cup juice
Oranges = 2 medium or 2/3 cup juice
Peaches = 4 medium or 2 cups sliced
Pears = 4 medium or 2 cups sliced
Pineapple = 1 1/2 cups pared, cubed
Potatoes = 2 1/4 cups diced; 1 3/4 cups mashed
Squash, winter = 1 cup, cooked
Squash, summer = 1 1/2 cups, cooked

INDEX

SUGGESTED REFERENCES
FOR DEHYDRATION INFORMATION

Bills, Jay and Shirley, *Home Food Dehydrating*. Bountiful, Utah. Horizon Publishers, 1974.

Carcione, Joe, and Lucas, Bob; *The Greengrocer*. New York, New York: Pyramid Communications, Inc., 1974.

Dickey, Esther, *Passport To Survival*. Salt Lake City: Bookcraft Publishers, 1969.

Hertzberg, Ruth; Vaugahn, Beatrice, and Green, Janet; *Putting Food By*. Brattleboro, Vermont: S. Greene Press, 1973.

Organic Gardening and Farming, *Stocking Up*. Ed. Carol Stoner. Emmaus, Pennsylvania: Rodale Press, 1973.

Sunset Books, *Home Canning*. Ed. Judith A. Gaulke. Menlo Park, California: Lane Publishing Company, 1975.